THIS BOOK BELONGS TO
Julia Black
926-1872.

BEST-LOVED VERSE

GOOD NIGHT AND GOOD MORNING *(page 202)*

GREAT, WIDE, BEAUTIFUL, WONDERFUL WORLD

(page 178)

BEST-LOVED VERSE

Illustrated by Margaret Tarrant

GALLERY BOOKS
An Imprint of W. H. Smith Publishers Inc.
112 Madison Avenue
New York City 10016

This edition published in 1990 by Gallery Books,
an imprint of W. H. Smith Publishers, Inc.,
112 Madison Avenue, New York, New York 10016
ISBN 0-8317-1364-X

Gallery Books are available for bulk purchase
for sales promotions and premium use.
For details write or telephone the
Manager of Special Sales, W. H. Smith Publishers, Inc.,
112 Madison Avenue, New York, New York 10016.
(212) 532-6600

Typeset by Litho Link Ltd, Welshpool, Wales
Printed and bound in Norway

BEST-LOVED VERSE

CONTENTS

IF NO ONE EVER MARRIES ME

If no one ever marries me–
  And I don't see why they should.
For nurse says I'm not pretty,
  And I'm seldom very good–

If no one ever marries me
  I shan't mind very much,
I shall buy a squirrel in a cage
  And a little rabbit-hutch;

I shall have a cottage near a wood,
  And a pony all my own,
And a little lamb, quite clean and tame,
  That I can take to town.

And when I'm getting really old–
  At twenty-eight or nine–
I shall buy a little orphan-girl
  And bring her up as mine.

Laurence Alma-Tadema

JACK FROST

Look out! look out!
  Jack Frost is about!
He's after our fingers and toes;
  And, all through the night,
  The quick little sprite
Is working when nobody knows.

  He'll climb each tree,
  So nimble is he,
His silvery powder he'll shake;
  To windows he'll creep,
  And while we're asleep,
Such wonderful pictures he'll make.

  Across the grass
  He'll merrily pass,
And change all its greenness to white;
  Then home he will go,
  And laugh, "Ho! ho! ho!
What fun I have had in the night!"

Cecily E. Pike

BABY SEED SONG

Little brown brother, oh! little brown brother,
Are you awake in the dark?
Here we lie cosily, close to each other;
Hark to the song of the lark!
"Waken!" the lark says, "waken and dress you;
Put on your green coats and gay:
Blue sky will shine on you, sunshine caress you–
Waken! 'Tis morning– 'tis May!"

Little brown brother, oh! little brown brother,
What kind of flower will you be?
I'll be a poppy–all white, like my mother;
Do be a poppy like me.
What! you're a sun-flower? How I shall miss you
When you're grown golden and high!
But I shall send all the bees up to kiss you,
Little brown brother, good-bye!

E. Nesbit

PIPPA'S SONG

The year's at the spring,
And day's at the morn;
Morning's at seven;
The hill-side's dew-pearled;
The lark's on the wing;
The snail's on the thorn;
God's in His heaven–
All's right with the world.

Robert Browning

GRACE FOR A CHILD

Here a little child I stand,
  Heaving up my either hand;
Cold as paddocks though they be,
  Here I lift them up to Thee,
For a benison to fall
On our meat, and on us all. Amen.

Robert Herrick

THE BARREL ORGAN

Go down to Kew in lilac-time, in lilac-time,
in lilac-time;
Go down to Kew in lilac-time (it isn't far
from London!),
And you shall wander hand-in-hand with love
in summer's wonderland:
Go down to Kew in lilac-time (it isn't far
from London!).

The cherry-trees are seas of bloom, and soft
perfume, and sweet perfume,
The cherry-trees are seas of bloom (and oh!
so near to London!),
And there they say, when dawn is high, and
all the world's a blaze of sky,
The cuckoo, though he's very shy, will sing
a song for London.

The nightingale is rather rare, and yet they
say you'll hear him there,
At Kew, at Kew, in lilac-time (and oh! so
near to London!),
The linnet and the throstle too, and after dark
the long halloo,
And golden-eyed *tu-whit, tu-whoo*, of owls
that ogle London.

For Noah hardly knew a bird of any kind that
isn't heard
At Kew, at Kew, in lilac-time (and oh! so
near to London!),
And when the rose begins to pout, and all the
chestnut spires are out,
You hear the rest without a doubt, all chorus-
ing for London:

Come down to Kew in lilac-time, in lilac-time,
in lilac-time;
Come down to Kew in lilac-time (it isn't far
from London!),
And you shall wander hand-in-hand with love
in summer's wonderland:
Come down to Kew in lilac-time (it isn't far
from London!).

Alfred Noyes

THE FIRST OF JUNE

The wind to west is steady,
  The weather is sweet and fair;
Laburnum, slender lady,
  Shakes out her yellow hair.

Magnolia, like a stranger,
  Stands stiffly all alone;
I think a word would change her
  Into a flower of stone.

The solid guelder roses
  Are white as dairy cream;
The hyacinths fade, like posies;
  The cloud hangs in a dream.

And dreams of light and shadow
  The sleeping meadow shake,
But the king-cup shines in the meadow,
  A gold eye wide awake.

William Brighty Rands

THE FIRST OF JUNE

PITTYPAT AND TIPPYTOE

PITTYPAT AND TIPPYTOE

All day long they come and go,–
Pittypat and Tippytoe;
  Footprints up and down the hall,
    Playthings scattered on the floor,
  Finger-marks along the wall,
    Tell-tale streaks upon the door,–
By these presents you shall know
Pittypat and Tippytoe.

How they riot at their play!
And a dozen times a day
  In they troop, demanding bread,–
    Only buttered bread will do.
  And that butter must be spread
    Inches thick with sugar too!
Never yet have I said, "No,
Pittypat and Tippytoe!"

Oh, the thousand worrying things
Every day recurrent brings!
  Hands to scrub and hair to brush,
    Search for playthings gone amiss,

continued on next page

Many a murmuring to hush,
Many a little bump to kiss;
Life's indeed a fleeting show,
Pittypat and Tippytoe!

And when day is at the end,
There are little duds to mend;
Little frocks are strangely torn,
Little shoes great holes reveal,
Little hose, but one day worn,
Rudely yawn at toe or heel!
Who but you could work such woe,
Pittypat and Tippytoe?

But when comes this thought to me,
"Some there are that childless be,"
Stealing to their little beds,
With a love I cannot speak,
Tenderly I stroke their heads,
Fondly kiss each velvet cheek.
God help those who do not know
A Pittypat or Tippytoe!

Eugene Field

GOD'S WORK

Cows in the meadow
And birds in the tree;
Horses on the highways
And fish in the sea;

Sailors in schooners,
And miners in mines,
Deep down in pits
Where the sun never shines;

Girls playing jin-go-ring,
Boys spinning tops;
Mothers in kitchens,
And fathers in shops;

The sun in the heavens
From morning to night,
Making the fields and flowers
Laugh in his light;

Watching o'er everything
All the day through;
Oh, what a lot of work
God has to do!

Gabriel Setoun

THE ELF AND THE DORMOUSE

Under a toadstool
Crept a wee elf
Out of the rain
To shelter himself.

Under the toadstool
Sound asleep
Sat a big dormouse
All in a heap.

Trembled the wee elf
Frightened, and yet
Fearing to fly away
Lest he got wet.

To the next shelter
Maybe a mile!
Sudden the wee elf
Smiled a wee smile,

Tugged till the toadstool
Toppled in two,
Holding it over him
Gaily he flew.

Soon he was safe home,
Dry as could be;
Soon woke the dormouse–
"Good gracious me!

"Where is my toadstool?"
Loud he lamented–
And that's how umbrellas
First were invented.

Oliver Herford

THE ROBIN

When father takes his spade to dig
  Then Robin comes along;
He sits upon a little twig
  And sings a little song.

Or, if the trees are rather far,
  He does not stay alone,
But comes up close to where we are
  And bobs up on a stone.

Laurence Alma-Tadema

PATER'S BATHE

You can take a tub with a rub and a scrub in
a two-foot tank of tin,
You can stand and look at the whirling brook
and think about jumping in;
You can chatter and shake in the cold black
lake, but the kind of bath for me,
Is to take a dip from the side of a ship, in the
trough of the rolling sea.

You may lie and dream in the bed of a stream
when an August day is dawning,
Or believe 'tis nice to break the ice on your tub
of a winter morning;
You may sit and shiver beside the river, but
the kind of bath for me,
Is to take a dip from the side of a ship, in the
trough of the rolling sea.

Judge Parry

HOW THE LITTLE KITE LEARNED TO FLY

"I never can do it," the little kite said,
As he looked at the others high over his head;
"I know I should fall if I tried to fly."
"Try," said the big kite; "only try!
Or I fear you will never learn at all."
But the little kite said, "I'm afraid I'll fall."

The big kite nodded: "Ah, well, good-bye;
I'm off"; and he rose toward the tranquil sky.
Then the little kite's paper stirred at the sight,
And, trembling, he shook himself free for flight.
First whirling and frightened, then braver grown,
Up, up he rose through the air alone,
Till the big kite looking down could see
The little one rising steadily.

Then how the little kite thrilled with pride,
As he sailed with the big kite side by side!
While far below he could see the ground,
And the boys like small spots moving round.
They rested high in the quiet air,
And only the birds and the clouds were there.
"Oh, how happy I am!" the little kite cried;
"And all because I was brave, and tried."

Anonymous

CHOOSING A NAME

I have got a new-born sister;
I was nigh the first that kissed her.
When the nursing woman brought her
To papa, his infant daughter,
How papa's dear eyes did glisten!–
She will shortly be to christen:
And papa has made the offer,
I shall have the naming of her.

Now I wonder what would please her,
Charlotte, Julia, or Louisa.
Ann and Mary, they're too common;
Joan's too formal for a woman;
Jane's a prettier name beside;
But we had a Jane that died.
They would say, if 'twas Rebecca,
That she was a little Quaker.
Edith's pretty, but that looks
Better in old English books;
Ellen's left off long ago;
Blanche is out of fashion now.
None that I have named as yet
Are so good as Margaret.
Emily is neat and fine.
What do you think of Caroline?

How I'm puzzled and perplexed
What to choose or think of next!
I am in a little fever.
Lest the name that I shall give her
Should disgrace her or defame her,
I will leave papa to name her.

Charles and Mary Lamb

ROUND AND ROUND

Round and round the garden
Like a teddy bear;
One step, two step,
Tickle you under there.

Anonymous

THE HORNY-GOLOCH

The Horny-Goloch is a fearsome beast,
Supple and scaly;
It has two horns, and a handful of feet,
And a forkie tailie!

Anonymous

THE FAIRY QUEEN

A little fairy comes at night,
Her eyes are blue, her hair is brown,
With silver spots upon her wings,
And from the moon she flutters down.

She has a little silver wand,
And when a good child goes to bed
She waves her hand from right to left,
And makes a circle round its head.

And then it dreams of pleasant things,
Of fountains filled with fairy fish,
And of trees that bear delicious fruit
And bow their branches at a wish:

Of arbours filled with dainty scents
From lovely flowers that never fade;
Bright flies that glitter in the sun,
And glow-worms shining in the shade:

And talking birds with gifted tongues,
For singing songs and telling tales,
And pretty dwarfs to show the way
Through fairy hills and fairy dales.

But when a bad child goes to bed,
From left to right she weaves her rings,
And then it dreams all through the night
Of only ugly horrid things!

Then lions come with glaring eyes,
And tigers growl, a dreadful noise,
And ogres draw their cruel knives,
To shed the blood of girls and boys.

Then stormy waves rush on to drown,
Or raging flames come scorching round,
Fierce dragons hover in the air,
And serpents crawl along the ground.

Then wicked children wake and weep,
And wish the long black gloom away;
But good ones love the dark, and find
The night as pleasant as the day.

Thomas Hood

ROBIN REDBREAST

Good-bye, good-bye to summer!
  For summer's nearly done;
The garden smiling faintly,
  Cool breezes in the sun:
Our thrushes now are silent,
  Our swallows flown away,–
But Robin's here in coat of brown,
  With ruddy breast-knot gay.
    Robin, Robin Redbreast,
    O Robin dear!
    Robin singing sweetly
      In the falling of the year.

Bright yellow, red and orange,
  The leaves come down in hosts;
The trees are Indian Princes,
  But soon they'll turn to Ghosts;
The scanty pears and apples
  Hang russet on the bough,
It's autumn, autumn, autumn late,
  'Twill soon be winter now.
    Robin, Robin Redbreast,
    O Robin dear!
    And weladay! my Robin,
      For pinching times are near.

The fireside for the cricket,
The wheatstack for the mouse,
When trembling night-winds whistle
And moan all round the house;
The frosty ways like iron,
The branches plumed with snow,–
Alas! in winter, dead and dark,
Where can poor Robin go?
Robin, Robin Redbreast,
O Robin dear!
And a crumb of bread for Robin,
His little heart to cheer.

William Allingham

WHETHER

Whether the weather be fine or whether
the weather be not,
Whether the weather be cold, or whether the
weather be hot,
We'll weather the weather, whatever the weather,
Whether we like it or not.

Anonymous

ON THE ROAD TO DREAMTOWN

Come here, my sleepy darling, and climb
upon my knee,
And lo! all in a moment, a trusted steed 'twill be
To bear you to that country where troubles are
forgot,
And we'll set off for Dreamtown, Trot–Trot–
Trot!

Oh, listen! Bells of Dreamland are ringing soft
and low!
What a pleasant, pleasant country it is through
which we go,
And little nodding travellers are seen in every
spot,
All riding off to Dreamtown, Trot–Trot–Trot!

The lights begin to twinkle above us in the sky,
The star-lamps that the angels are hanging out
on high
To guide the drowsy travellers where danger
lurketh not,
As they ride off to Dreamtown, Trot–Trot–
Trot!

Snug in a wild-rose cradle the warm wind rocks
the bee;
The little birds are sleeping in every bush and tree.
I wonder what they dream of? They dream and
answer not,
As we ride by to Dreamtown, Trot–Trot–Trot!

Our journey's almost over. The sleepy town's
in sight,
Wherein my drowsy darling must tarry over-
night.
How still it is, how peaceful, in this delightful spot,
As we ride into Dreamtown, Trot–Trot–Trot!

Eben E. Rexford

A DANISH CRADLE-SONG

Lullaby, sweet baby mine!
Mother spins the thread so fine;
Father o'er the long bridge is gone,
Shoes he'll buy for little John.
Pretty shoes with buckles bright.
Sleep, baby mine, now sleep all night!

Traditional

MY SHADOW

I have a little shadow, that goes in and
out with me,
And what can be the use of him is more than
I can see.
He is very, very like me from the heels up to
the head;
And I see him jump before me when I jump
into my bed.

The funniest thing about him is the way he
likes to grow–
Not at all like proper children, which is always
very slow;
But he sometimes shoots up taller, like an
india-rubber ball,
And he sometimes gets so little that there's
none of him at all.

He hasn't got a notion of how children ought
to play,
And can only make a fool of me in every sort
of way.
He stands so close beside me, he's a coward
you can see;
I'd think shame to stick to nursie as that
shadow sticks to me!

continued on page 39

MY SHADOW

THE BEE

One morning, very early, before the sun was
up,
I rose and found the shining dew on every
buttercup;
But my lazy little shadow, like an arrant sleepy-
head,
Had stayed at home behind me and was fast
asleep in bed.

Robert Louis Stevenson

THE BEE

There is a little gentleman
That wears the yellow trews,
A dirk below his doublet,
For sticking of his foes.

He's in a stinging posture
Where'er you do him see,
And if you offer violence
He'll stab his dirk in thee.

Anonymous

MOOLY COW

"Mooly cow, mooly cow, home from the wood,
They sent me to fetch you as fast as I could.
The sun has gone down, it is time to go home.
Mooly cow, mooly cow, why don't you come?
Your udders are full, and the milkmaid is there,
And the children all waiting their supper to share.
I have let the long bars down,–why don't you
pass through?"
The mooly cow only said, "Moo–o–o!"

"Mooly cow, mooly cow, have you not been
Regaling all day where the pastures are green?
No doubt it was pleasant, dear mooly, to see
The clear-running brook and the wide-spreading tree,
The clover to crop, and the streamlet to wade,
To drink the clear water and lie in the shade;
But now it is night; they are waiting for you."
The mooly cow only said, "Moo–o–o!"

"Mooly cow, mooly cow, where do you go,
When all the green pastures are covered with snow?
You go to the barn, and we feed you with hay,
And the maid goes to milk you there every day;
She pats you, she loves you, she strokes your
  sleek hide,
She speaks to you kindly, and sits by your side:
Then come along home, pretty mooly cow, do."
  The mooly cow only said, "Moo–o–o!"

"Mooly cow, mooly cow, whisking your tail,
The milkmaid is waiting, I say, with her pail;
She tucks up her petticoats, tidy and neat,
And places the three-leggèd stool for her seat:–
What can you be staring at, mooly? You know
That we ought to have gone home an hour ago.
How dark it is growing! Oh, what shall I do?"
  The mooly cow only said, "Moo–o–o!"

Anna M. Wells

THE DUST-MAN

When the shades of night are falling, and
the sun goes down,
Oh! the Dust-man comes a-creeping in from
Shut-eye Town.
And he throws dust in the eyes of all the babies
that he meets,
No matter where he finds them, in the house or
in the streets.
Then the baby's eyes grow heavy and the lids
drop down,
When the Dust-man comes a-creeping in from
Shut-eye Town.

When Mother lights the lamp and draws the
curtains down,
Oh! the Dust-man comes a-creeping in from
Shut-eye Town,
And the babies think the Dust-man is as mean
as he can be,
For he shuts their eyes at nightfall just when
they want to see.

But their little limbs are weary, for they all
fret and frown,
When the Dust-man comes a-creeping in from
Shut-eye Town.

Anonymous

UNLESS

"I wish, I wish I were a fish,"
  Said Bobbie to his sister,
As in his net he chanced to get
  A little speckled twister

"Precisely so," the fish replied,
  As he kept twisting faster,
"Unless you find in your inside
  A hook, my little master."

"I wish, I wish I were a fish,
  With all my dear relations;
No need to go to school, you know,
  And never do dictations.
And never have to wash or dress,
  And never to be beaten!"

"Quite so," the fish remarked, "unless
  You happen to be eaten!"

Fred E. Weatherly

A LULLABY

Baby, baby, hush-a-bye,
  Must you be awake now?
Sweet my lamb, come, close your eye,
  Sleep for mother's sake now.

Baby mice are safe from harm
  In their downy holes now:
Baby squirrels lie all warm
  In the hollow boles now.

Baby buds are fast asleep
  Rocking on the trees now:
Baby fishes, far and deep,
  Slumber in the seas now.

All the baby stars above
  Dream in cloudy bed now:
Mother Moon, for all her love,
  Sleeping hides her head now.

Baby, baby, hush-a-bye,
  Cradled on my breast now,
Sweet my lamb, come, close your eye,
  Let your mother rest now.

Laurence Alma-Tadema

JEMIMA

There was a little girl who had a little curl,
Right in the middle of her forehead,
And when she was good, she was very, very good,
But when she was bad she was horrid.

One day she went upstairs, while her parents,
  unawares,
In the kitchen down below were occupied with meals,
And she stood upon her head, on her little truckle bed,
And she then began drumming with her heels.

Her mother heard the noise, and thought it was the
  boys,
A-playing at a combat in the attic,
But when she climbed the stair and saw Jemima there,
She took and she did smack her most emphatic!

Anonymous

BUTTERCUPS AND DAISIES

Buttercups and Daisies,
  Oh! the pretty flowers!
Coming ere the spring-time,
  To tell of sunny hours.
While the trees are leafless,
  While the fields are bare,
Buttercups and Daisies
  Spring up everywhere.

Little hardy flowers,
  Like to children poor,
Playing in their sturdy health,
  By their mother's door.
Purple with the north wind,
  Yet alert and bold,
Fearing not, and caring not,
  Though they be a-cold.

What to them is weather?
  What are stormy showers?
Buttercups and Daises,
  Are these human flowers!
He who gave them hardship,
  And a life of care,
Gave them likewise hardy strength,
  And patient hearts to bear!

Welcome, yellow Buttercups!
  Welcome, Daisies white!
Ye are in my spirit
  Visioned, a delight!
Coming ere the spring-time
  Of sunny hours to tell:–
Speaking to our hearts of Him
  Who doeth all things well.

Mary Howitt

IF I WERE AN APPLE

If I were an apple,
And grew on a tree,
I think I'd drop down
On a nice boy like me.
I wouldn't stay there,
Giving nobody joy;
I'd fall down at once
And say, "Eat me, my boy!"

Anonymous

THE MONTHS

January brings the snow,
Makes our feet and fingers glow.

February brings the rain,
Thaws the frozen lake again.

March brings breezes loud and shrill,
Stirs the dancing daffodil.

April brings the promise sweet,
Scatters daisies at our feet.

May brings flocks of pretty lambs,
Skipping by their fleecy dams.

June brings tulips, lilies, roses,
Fills the children's hands with posies.

Hot July brings cooling showers,
Apricots and gillyflowers.

August brings the sheaves of corn,
Then the harvest home is borne.

Warm September brings the fruit,
Sportsmen then begin to shoot.

Fresh October brings the pheasant,
Then to gather nuts is pleasant.

Dull November brings the blast,
Then the leaves are whirling fast.

Chill December brings the sleet,
Blazing fire and Christmas treat.

Sara Coleridge

BARTHOLOMEW

Bartholomew
  Is very sweet,
From sandy hair
  To rosy feet.

Bartholomew
  Is six months old,
And dearer far
  Than pearls or gold.

Bartholomew
  Is hugged and kissed!
He loves a flower
  In either fist.

Bartholomew's
  My saucy son:
No mother has
  A sweeter one!

Norman Gale

THE BLIND MEN AND THE ELEPHANT

It was six men of Hindostan,
To learning much inclined,
Who went to see the elephant,
(Though all of them were blind);
That each by observation
Might satisfy his mind.

The first approached the elephant,
And happening to fall
Against his broad and sturdy side,
At once began to bawl,
"Bless me, it seems the elephant
Is very like a wall."

The second, feeling of his tusk,
Cried, "Ho! what have we here
So very round and smooth and sharp?
To me 'tis mighty clear
This wonder of an elephant
Is very like a spear."

The third approached the animal,
And happening to take
The squirming trunk within his hands,
Then boldly up and spake;
"I see," quoth he, "the elephant
Is very like a snake."

The fourth stretched out his eager hand
And felt about the knee,
"What most this mighty beast is like
Is mighty plain," quoth he;
" 'Tis clear enough the elephant
Is very like a tree."

The fifth who chanced to touch the ear
Said, "Even the blindest man
Can tell what this resembles most;
Deny the fact who can,
This marvel of an elephant
Is very like a fan."

The sixth no sooner had begun
About the beast to grope
Than, seizing on the swinging tail
That fell within his scope,
"I see," cried he, "the elephant
Is very like a rope."

And so these men of Hindostan
Disputed loud and long,
Each in his own opinion
Exceeding stiff and strong,
Though *each* was *partly* in the right,
And *each* was *partly* wrong.

J. G. Saxe

THE STARS

Each night, before I go to sleep,
I look between the bars
That make the nursery window safe,
And gaze up at the stars.

They twinkle and they smile at me
As if they meant to say,
"Good-night! sleep well, 'tis now our turn
To run about and play."

One night a star fell out of bed:
It fell from such a height,
I'm sure it must have hurt itself
And had an awful fright.

I love the stars, they look so kind,
High up there in the skies,
Like little lamps God hangs in Heaven–
Or p'raps they're angels' eyes.

Alethea Chaplin

LITTLE BROWN HOUSES

Little brown houses, now what do you hold?
Treasures of purple, and crimson, and gold?
Kings, queens, and princesses wear robes like these,
Tell us who live in you, brown houses, please!

See! the doors open, and now can be seen
Dear little waiting-men, dress'd all in green,
Daily they climb higher into the air,
What are they guarding with such tender care?

Ah! now we know, for the secret is out,
Flowers, spring flowers, are all round about,
These were the treasures the brown houses kept,
Safe from all harm while through winter they slept.

Here is King Daffodil, golden and gay,
There is Queen Hyacinth not far away,
There are the princesses, crocuses small,
God is the maker and giver of all.

Cecily E. Pike

TARTARY

If I were Lord of Tartary,
  Myself and me alone,
My bed should be of ivory,
  Of beaten gold my throne;
And in my court should peacocks flaunt,
And in my forests tigers haunt,
And in my pools great fishes slant
  Their fins athwart the sun.

If I were Lord of Tartary,
  Trumpeters every day
To all my meals should summon me,
  And in my courtyards bray;
And in the evenings lamps should shine
Yellow as honey, red as wine,
While harp and flute and mandoline
  Made music sweet and gay.

If I were Lord of Tartary,
  I'd wear a robe of beads,
White, and gold, and green they'd be–
  And small, and thick as seeds;
And ere should wane the morning star,
I'd don my robe and scimitar,
And zebras seven should draw my car
  Through Tartary's dark glades.

Walter De La Mare

IF I WERE LORD OF TARTARY

A CHILD'S THOUGHT OF GOD

A CHILD'S THOUGHT OF GOD

They say that God lives very high!
But if you look above the pines
You cannot see our God. And why?

And if you dig down in the mines,
You never see Him in the gold,
Though from Him all that's glory shines.

God is so good, He wears a fold
Of Heaven and earth across His face,
Like secrets kept, for love untold.

But still I feel that His embrace
Slides down by thrills, through all things made,
Through sight and sound of every place:

As if my tender mother laid
On my shut lids, her kisses' pressure,
Half-waking me at night; and said,
"Who kissed you in the dark, dear guesser?"

Elizabeth Barrett Browning

FANNY

Little Miss Fanny,
So cubic and canny,
With blues eyes and blue shoes–
The Queen of the Blues!
As darling a girl as there is in the world–
If she'll laugh, skip and jump,
And not be Miss Glump!

Samuel Taylor Coleridge

THE DANDELION

"Dandelion, what's o'clock?"
At your door now hear us knock;
White and feathery you are growing,
Calling to the breezes blowing,
"Take my baby seeds, I pray,
Gently blow them far away."

One, Two, Three, Four;
Now she opens wide her door.
See! the baby seeds are flying,
In the earth they'll soon be lying;
Such a pretty sight will be,
When the golden flowers we see.

Cecily E. Pike

A GRACE BEFORE DINNER

O Thou, who kindly dost provide
For every creature's want!
We bless Thee, God of Nature wide,
For all Thy goodness lent.
And, if it please Thee, Heavenly Guide,
May never worse be sent;
But, whether granted or denied,
Lord, bless us with content. Amen.

Robert Burns

INSIDE OUT

Though outwardly a gloomy shroud,
The inner half of every cloud
   Is bright and shining:
I therefore turn my clouds about
And always wear them inside out
   To show the lining.

Ellen Thorneycroft Fowler

THE KNIGHT'S PRAYER

God be in my head
And in my understanding;

God be in my eyes
And in my looking;

God be in my mouth
And in my speaking;

God be in my heart
And in my thinking;

God be at my end
And at my departing.

Traditional

THE WAY THROUGH THE WOODS

They shut the road through the woods
Seventy years ago.
Weather and rain have undone it again,
And now you would never know

There was once a road through the woods
Before they planted the trees.
It is underneath the coppice and heath,
And the thin anemones.
Only the keeper sees
That, where the ring dove broods,
And the badgers roll at ease,
There was once a road through the woods.

Yet, if you enter the woods
Of a summer evening late,
When the night-air cools on the trout-ringed pools
Where the otter whistles his mate,
(They fear not men in the woods,
Because they see so few.)
You will hear the beat of a horse's feet,
And the swish of a skirt in the dew,
Steadily cantering through
The misty solitudes,
As though they perfectly knew
The old lost road through the woods . . .
But there is no road through the woods.

Rudyard Kipling

TO BE RID OF CARE

What shall we do to be rid of care?
Pack up her best clothes and pay her fare;

Pay her fare and let her go
By an early train to Jer–i–cho.

There in Judea she will be
Slumbering under a green palm-tree;

And the Arabs of the Desert will come round
When they see her lying on the ground.

And some will say, "Did you ever see
Such a remark–a–bil babee?"

And others in the language the Arabs use,
"Nous n'avons jamais vu une telle papoose!"

And she will grow and grow, and then
She will marry a chief of the Desert Men;

And he will keep her from heat and cold,
And deck her in silk and satin and gold–

With bangles for her feet and jewels for her hair,
And other articles that ladies wear!

So pack up her best clothes and let her go
By an early train to Jer–i–cho!

Pack up her best clothes and pay her fare;
So *we* shall be rid of trouble and care!

William Canton

THE ALL ALONE TREE

There's a tree that is growing alone on the hill,
By the path that winds up at the back of the mill,
And we're awfully fond of it, Maudie and me,
And we call it the All Alone, All Alone Tree.

It's old, and it's wrinkled and twisted and dry,
And it grows by itself with no other tree nigh,
And we always sit under it, Maudie and me,
Because it's the All Alone, All Alone Tree.

In the bright summer-time when they're cutting the hay,
Then the birds come and sing in its branches all day,
And we're awfully glad of this, Maudie and me,
Because it's the All Alone, All Alone Tree.
But in the dark winter the birds have all flown,
And we know that it's standing there, quite, quite alone,
So we creep out and kiss it then, Maudie and me,
Because it's the All Alone, All Alone Tree.

F. O'Neill Gallagher

THE STORY OF AUGUSTUS WHO WOULD NOT HAVE ANY SOUP

Augustus was a chubby lad;
Fat, ruddy cheeks Augustus had;
And everybody saw with joy
The plump and hearty, healthy boy.
He ate and drank as he was told,
And never let his soup grow cold.
But one day, one cold winter's day,
He screamed out– "Take the soup away!
Oh, take the nasty soup away!
I won't have any soup to-day."

Next day begins his tale of woes,
Quite lank and lean Augustus grows.
Yet though he feels so weak and ill,
The naughty fellow cries out still–
"Not any soup for me, I say:
Oh, take the nasty soup away!
I won't have any soup to-day."

The third day comes; oh, what a sin,
To make himself so pale and thin!
Yet, when the soup is put on table,
He screams as loud as he is able–

"Not any soup for me, I say:
Oh, take the nasty soup away!
I won't have any soup to-day."

Look at him, now the fourth day's come!
He scarcely weighs a sugar plum;
He's like a little bit of thread,
And on the fifth day, he was–dead!

Dr. Heinrich Hoffmann

THE NESTING HOUR

Robin-Friend has gone to bed,
Little wing to hide his head–
Mother's bird must slumber too
Just as baby Robins do–
When the stars begin to rise,
Birds and babies close their eyes.

Laurence Alma-Tadema

THE OLD KITCHEN CLOCK

Listen to the kitchen clock!
  To itself it ever talks,
  From its place it never walks:
"Tick-tock–tick-tock!"
  Tell me what it says.

"I'm a very patient clock,
  Never moved by hope or fear,
  Though I've stood for many a year,
Tick-tock–tick-tock!"
  That is what it says.

"I'm a very truthful clock:
  People say about the place
  Truth is written on my face:
Tick-tock–tick-tock!"
  That is what it says.

"I'm a very active clock,
  For I go while you're asleep,
  Though you never take a peep;
Tick-tock–tick-tock!"
  That is what it says.

"I'm a most obliging clock:
If you wish to hear me strike,
You may do it when you like;
Tick-tock–tick-tock!"
That is what it says.

What a talkative old clock!
Let us see what it will do
When the pointer reaches two;
"Ding-dong!–Tick-tock!"
That is what it says.

Anne Hawkshaw

I WOULD LIKE YOU FOR A COMRADE

I would like you for a comrade, for I love
you, that I do,
I never met a little girl as amiable as you;
I would teach you how to dance and sing and
how to talk and laugh,
If I were not a little girl and you were not a calf.

continued on next page

I would like you for a comrade, you should
 share my barley meal,
And butt me with your little horns just hard
 enough to feel;
We would lie beneath the chestnut-trees and
 watch the leaves uncurl,
If I were not a clumsy calf and you a little girl.

Judge Parry

A BOY'S ASPIRATIONS

I was four yesterday: when I'm quite old,
I'll have a cricket-ball made of pure gold;
I'll carve the roast meat, and help soup and fish;
I'll get my feet wet whenever I wish.

I'll spend a hundred pounds every day;
I'll have the alphabet quite done away;
I'll have a parrot without a sharp beak;
I'll see a pantomine six times a week.

I'll have a rose-tree always in bloom;
I'll keep a dancing bear in mamma's room;
I'll spoil my best clothes, and not care a pin;
I'll have no visitors ever let in.

I'll go at liberty upstairs or down;
I'll pin a dishcloth to the cook's gown;
I'll light the candles, and ring the big bell;
I'll smoke papa's pipe, feeling quite well.

I'll have a ball of string fifty miles long;
I'll have a whistle as loud as the gong;
I'll scold the housemaid for making a dirt;
I'll cut my fingers without being hurt.

I'll never stand up to show that I'm grown;
No one shall say to me, "Don't throw a stone!"
I'll drop my buttered toast on the new chintz;
I'll have no governess giving her hints!

I'll have a nursery up in the stars;
I'll lean through windows without any bars;
I'll sail without my nurse in a big boat;
I'll have no comforters tied round my throat.

I'll have a language with not a word spell'd;
I'll ride on horseback without being held;
I'll hear mamma say, "My boy, good as gold!"
When I'm a grown-up man sixty years old.

Menella Bute Smedley

LADY MOON

"Lady Moon, Lady Moon, where are you roving?"
"Over the sea."
"Lady Moon, Lady Moon, whom are you loving?"
"All that love me."

"Are you not tired with rolling, and never
Resting to sleep?
Why look so pale and so sad, as forever
Wishing to weep?"

"Ask me not this, little child, if you love me.
You are too bold.
I must obey my dear Father above me,
And do as I'm told."

"Lady Moon, Lady Moon, where are you roving?"
"Over the sea."
"Lady Moon, Lady Moon, whom are you loving?"
"All that love me."

Lord Houghton

BUBBLE-BLOWING

Our plot is small, but sunny limes
  Shut out all cares and troubles;
And there my little girl at times
  And I sit blowing bubbles.

They glide, they dart, they soar, they break.
  Oh, joyous little daughter,
What lovely coloured worlds we make,
  What crystal flowers of water!

One, green and rosy, slowly drops;
  One soars and shines a minute,
And carries to the lime-tree tops
  Our home, reflected in it.

The gable, with cream rose in bloom,
  She sees from roof to basement;
"Oh, father, there's your little room!"
  She cries in glad amazement.

Tell what we did, and how we played,
  Withdrawn from care and trouble–
A father and his merry maid,
  Whose house was in a bubble.

William Canton

THE LAND OF STORY BOOKS

At evening when the lamp is lit,
Around the fire my parents sit;
They sit at home and talk and sing,
And do not play at anything.

Now, with my little gun, I crawl
All in the dark along the wall,
And follow round the forest track
Away behind the sofa back.

There, in the night, where none can spy,
All in my hunter's camp I lie,
And play at books that I have read
Till it is time to go to bed.

I see the others far away
As if in firelit camp they lay,
And I, like to an Indian scout,
Around their party prowled about.

So, when my nurse comes in for me,
Home I return across the sea,
And go to bed with backward looks
At my dear land of Story books.

Robert Louis Stevenson

THE LAND OF STORY BOOKS

OUR CAT

OUR CAT

Oh, I wish that you had seen him,
Our little pussy-cat,
He came so skinny, scrag, and lean,
And went away so fat.
They said he stole the food and things,
Perhaps hc did so, but,
He really couldn't help it,
Couldn't Smut.

He walked upon the dresser-shelf,
And knocked down mother's jugs;
Broke half-a-dozen dinner plates,
And Kate's and Molly's mugs.
I guess he thought he heard a mouse;
He did not catch it, but,
He really couldn't help it,
Couldn't Smut.

At night he went upon the spree,
And danced upon the tiles,
His caterwaul re-echoing round,
For miles, and miles, and miles.
Poor Pater said it woke him up,
No doubt it did so, but,
He really couldn't help it,
Couldn't Smut.

continued on next page

He tore up half the leather chairs,
They bought a set to match,
And just to show he noticed it,
He marked them with a scratch.
Then Pater he was raging mad;
It was annoying, but,
He really couldn't help it,
Couldn't Smut.

So of fellowship and feelings too,
We made a sacrifice,
And gave him to a farmer-man,
To catch his rats and mice.
We wept to lose our pussy-cat,
And he was sorry, but,
We really couldn't help it,
Could we, Smut?

Judge Parry

THE SECRET PLAYMATE

When I am playing underneath the tree,
I look around–and there he is with me!

Among the shadows of the boughs he stands,
And shakes the leaves at me with both his hands.

And then upon the mossy roots we lie,
And watch the leaves make pictures on the sky.

And then we swing and float from bough to bough–
And never fall? I can't remember how.

The games I play with him are always best,
And yet we cannot teach them to the rest.

For when the others come to join our play
I look around–and he has slipped away!

They ask me if he speaks–I cannot tell,
But no one else can play with me so well.

Josephine Daskam Bacon

THE DREAM OF A BOY WHO LIVED AT NINE-ELMS

Nine grenadiers, with bayonets in their guns;
Nine bakers' baskets, with hot-cross buns;
Nine brown elephants, standing in a row;
Nine new velocipedes, good ones to go;
Nine knickerbocker suits, with buttons all complete;
Nine pairs of skates, with straps for the feet;
Nine clever conjurers eating hot coals;
Nine sturdy mountaineers leaping on their poles;
Nine little drummer-boys beating on their drums;
Nine fat aldermen sitting on their thumbs;
Nine new knockers to our front door;
Nine new neighbours that I never saw before;
Nine times running I dreamt it all plain;
With bread and cheese for supper I could
  dream it all again.

William Brighty Rands

THE DREAM OF A GIRL WHO LIVED AT SEVEN-OAKS

Seven sweet singing birds up in a tree;
Seven swift sailing-ships white upon the sea;
Seven bright weather-cocks shining in the sun;
Seven slim race-horses ready for a run;
Seven gold butterflies, flitting overhead;
Seven red roses blowing in a garden-bed;
Seven white lilies, with honey bees inside them;
Seven round rainbows with clouds to divide them;
Seven pretty little girls with sugar on their lips;
Seven witty little boys, whom everybody tips;
Seven nice fathers, to call little maids joys;
Seven nice mothers, to kiss the little boys;
Seven nights running I dreamt it all plain;
With bread and jam for supper I could
  dream it all again.

William Brighty Rands

THE SONG OF THE WOODEN-LEGGED FIDDLER

I lived in a cottage adown in the West
When I was a boy, a boy;
But I knew no peace and I took no rest
Though the roses nigh smothered my snug little nest;
  For the smell of the sea
  Was much rarer to me,
And the life of a sailor was all my joy.

  Chorus–*The life of a sailor was all my joy!*

My mother she wept, and she begged me to stay
  Anchored for life to her apron-string,
And soon she would want me to help wi' the hay;
So I bided my time, then I flitted away
  On a night of delight in the following spring,
    With a pair of stout shoon
    And a seafaring tune
And a bundle and stick in the light of the moon,
    Down the long road
    To Portsmouth I strode,
To fight like a sailor for country and king.

Chorus–*To fight like a sailor for country and king!*

And now that my feet are turned homeward again
My heart is still crying, "Ahoy! Ahoy!"
And my thoughts are still out on the Spanish main
A-chasing the frigates of France and Spain,
For at heart an old sailor is always a boy;
And his nose will itch
For the powder and pitch
Till the days when he can't tell t'other from which,
Nor a grin o' the guns from a glint o' the sea,
Nor a skipper like Nelson from lubbers like me.

Chorus–*Nor a skipper like Nelson from lubbers like me!*

Ay! Now that I'm old I'm as bold as the best,
And the life of a sailor is all my joy;
Though I've swapped my leg
For a wooden peg
And my head is as bald as a new-laid egg,
The smell of the sea,
Is like victuals to me,
And I think in the grave I'll be crying, "Ahoy!"
For, though my old carcase is ready to rest,
At heart an old sailor is always a boy.

Chorus–*At heart an old sailor is always a boy.*

Alfred Noyes

SMILE

Smile, smile, smile, it's well worth while;
For while you smile another smiles,
And smiles come quick in piles and piles,
And soon there are miles and miles of smiles,
And life's worth while, if you smile, smile, smile.

Anonymous

NOWHERE

Do you know where the summer blooms all the year round,
Where there never is rain on a picnic day,
Where the thornless rose in its beauty grows,
And the little boys never are called from play?
Oh! hey! it is far away,
In the wonderful Land of Nowhere.

Would you like to live where nobody scolds,
Where you never are told, "It is time for bed,"
Where you learn without trying, and laugh without crying,
Where nurses don't pull when they comb your head?
Then oh! hey! you must hie away
To the wonderful Land of Nowhere.

If you long to dwell where you never need wait,
Where no one is punished or made to cry,
Where a supper of cakes is not followed by aches,
And little folks thrive on a diet of pie:
Then ho! hey! you must go, I say,
To the wonderful Land of Nowhere.

You must drift down the river of Idle Dreams,
Close to the border of No Man's Land;
For a year and a day you must sail away,
And then you will come to an unknown strand,
And ho! hey! if you get there–stay
In the wonderful Land of Nowhere.

Ella Wheeler Wilcox

LITTLE DROPS OF WATER

Little drops of water,
Little grains of sand,
Make the mighty ocean
And the pleasant land.

Thus the little minutes,
Humble though they be,
Make the mighty ages
Of eternity.

Anonymous

LUCY GRAY

Oft I had heard of Lucy Gray:
And, when I crossed the wild,
I chanced to see at break of day
The solitary child.

No mate, no comrade Lucy knew;
She dwelt on a wide moor,
–The sweetest thing that ever grew
Beside a human door!

You yet may spy the fawn at play,
The hare upon the green;
But the sweet face of Lucy Gray
Will never more be seen.

'Tonight will be a stormy night–
You to the town must go;
And take a lantern, child, to light
Your mother through the snow.'

'That, Father, will I gladly do:
'Tis scarcely afternoon–
The minster-clock has just struck two,
And yonder is the moon!'

At this the father raised his hook,
And snapped a faggot-band;
He plied his work; and Lucy took
The lantern in her hand.

Not blither is the mountain roe:
With many a wanton stroke
Her feet disperse the powdery snow,
That rises up like smoke.

The storm came on before its time:
She wandered up and down;
And many a hill did Lucy climb:
But never reached the town.

The wretched parents all that night
Went shouting far and wide;
But there was neither sound nor sight
To serve them for a guide.

At daybreak on a hill they stood
That overlooked the moor;
And thence they saw the bridge of wood,
A furlong from their door.

They wept–and, turning homeward, cried,
'In heaven we all shall meet';

continued on next page

–When in the snow the mother spied
The print of Lucy's feet.

Then downwards from the steep hill's edge
They tracked the footmarks small;
And through the broken hawthorn hedge,
And by the long stone-wall;

And then an open field they crossed:
The marks were still the same;
They tracked them on, nor ever lost;
And to the bridge they came.

They followed from the snowy bank
Those footmarks, one by one,
Into the middle of the plank;
And further there were none!

–Yet some maintain that to this day
She is a living child;
That you may see sweet Lucy Gray
Upon the lonesome wild.

O'er rough and smooth she trips along,
And never looks behind;
And sings a solitary song
That whistles in the wind.

William Wordsworth

THE BABY OVER THE WAY

"The Baby over the way, I know,
  Is a better Baby than me;
For the Baby over the way is all
  That a Baby ought to be.

"The Baby over the way is neat,
  When I'm not fit to be seen;
His frock is smooth and his bib is sweet,
  And his ears are always clean.

"He's wide awake when he's put to bed,
  But *he* never screams or cries;
He lies as still as a mouse, 'tis said,
  And closes his beautiful eyes.

"*He* never wanted a comforter,
  Nor sips of tea from a spoon;
He never crumpled his pinafore,
  He never cried for the moon.

"He's a dear little, sweet little angel bright,
  A love and a dove, they say;
But when I grow up, I am going to fight
  With the Baby over the way!"

Fay Inchfawn

SHUT THE DOOR

Godfrey Gordon Gustavus Gore–
No doubt you have heard the name before–
Was a boy who never would shut the door.

The wind might whistle, the wind might roar,
The teeth be aching and throats be sore;
But still he never would shut the door.

His father would beg, his mother implore,
"Godfrey Gordon Gustavus Gore,
We really wish you would shut the door!"

When he walked forth, the folks would roar,
"Godfrey Gordon Gustavus Gore,
Can't you remember to shut the door?"

They rigged out a shutter with sail and oar,
And threatened to pack off Gustavus Gore
On a voyage of penance to Singapore.

But he begged for mercy, and said, "No more!
Pray do not send me to Singapore
On a shutter, and then I will shut the door!"

"You will?" said his parents. "Then keep on shore!
But mind you do! For the plague is sore
Of a fellow that never will shut the door–
Godfrey Gordon Gustavus Gore."

Anonymous

LITTLE LOUISA

I wish every child was as good and polite
And contented as little Louisa.
At lessons or play, at all hours of the day,
There is nothing appears to displease her.

In summer the weather is never too warm,
No flies ever worry or tease her;
And if a big spider should sit down beside her
It wouldn't scare little Louisa.

In winter she never complains of the cold–
If Jack Frost endeavours to seize her
By the tip of her nose or her ten little toes
"I *like* chilblains," says little Louisa.

When she goes to the dentist–whom most people hate–
And he pulls out a tooth with his tweezers,
In spite of the pain, she says, "Do it again."
Oh! why can't we *all* be Louisas?

Ada Leonora Harris

CHILD'S SONG IN SPRING

The silver birch is a dainty lady,
  She wears a satin gown;
The elm tree makes the old churchyard shady,
  He will not live in town.

The English oak is a sturdy fellow,
  He gets his green coat late;
The willow is smart in a suit of yellow,
  While the brown beech trees wait.

Such a gay green gown God gives the larches–
  As green as He is good!
The hazels hold up their arms for arches
  When Spring rides through the wood.

The chestnut's proud and the lilac's pretty,
  The poplar's gentle and tall,
But the plane-tree is kind to the poor dull city–
  I love him best of all!

E. Nesbit

CHILD'S SONG IN SPRING

THE ROCK-A-BY LADY

THE ROCK-A-BY LADY

The Rock-a-by Lady from Hushaby Street
  Comes stealing, comes creeping;
The poppies they hang from her head to her feet,
And each hath a dream that is tiny and fleet–
She bringeth her poppies to you, my sweet,
  When she findeth you sleeping!

There is one little dream of a beautiful drum–
  "Rub-a-dub!" it goeth;
There is one little dream of a big sugar-plum,
And lo! thick and fast the other dreams come
Of pop-guns that bang, and tin tops that hum,
  And a trumpet that bloweth!

And dollies peep out of those wee little dreams
  With laughter and singing;
And boats go a-floating on silvery streams,
And the stars peek-a-boo with their own misty gleams,
And up, up, and up, where the Mother Moon beams,
  The fairies go winging!

Would you dream all these dreams that are tiny and fleet?
  They'll come to you sleeping;
So shut the two eyes that are weary, my sweet,
For the Rock-a-by Lady from Hushaby Street,
With poppies that hang from her head to her feet,
  Comes stealing; comes creeping.

Eugene Field

THE TALE OF A DOG AND A BEE

Great big dog,
  Head upon his toes;
Tiny little bee
  Settles on his nose.

Great big dog
  Thinks it is a fly,
Never says a word,
  Winks very sly.

Tiny little bee
  Tickles dog's nose–
Thinks like as not
  'Tis a pretty rose.

Dog smiles a smile,
  Winks his other eye,
Chuckles to himself
  How he'll catch a fly.

Then he makes a snap,
  Very quick and spry,
Gets the little bug,
  But doesn't catch the fly.

Tiny little bee,
  Alive and looking well,
Great big dog,
  Mostly gone to swell.

MORAL

Dear friends and brothers all,
Don't be too fast and free,
And when you catch a fly
Be sure it's not a bee.

Anonymous

A FAREWELL

My fairest child, I have no song to give you;
No lark could pipe to skies so dull and gray;
Yet, ere we part, one lesson I can leave you
For every day.
Be good, sweet maid, and let who will be clever,
Do noble things, nor dream them, all day long;
And so make life, death, and that vast for-ever
One grand, sweet song.

Charles Kingsley

WISHES

I wish I was a lily white,
A yellow rose or poppy red,
That when the day gave place to night
I should not have to go to bed.

I wish I was the Firth of Tay,
An armchair or a china cup,
That when the night turned into day
I need not bother to get up.

L. Elise

WALKING TO SCHOOL

Now I am five, my father says
  (And what he says you've got to mind)
That mother's not to hold my hand,
  Or even follow me behind,

To see I'm safe. But down the road,
  And all the way up the next street,
I am to walk now quite alone,
  No matter what the things I meet.

Still, five is really very old;
  It's pretty close to being a man.
Since I a soldier wish to be,
  I s'pose it's time that I began.

I'll swell my chest right out, like this,
  And swing my books behind, just so,
And wear my hat stuck sideways on,
  And whistle all the way I go.

There is a little boy I pass,
  He's always swinging on the gate,
He'll think that I am very old–
  Perhaps he'll think I'm seven, or eight.

There is a little girl I see,
  She'd always standing at her door,
When I come whistling boldly past,
  She'll wish that she were more than four.

What I mind most of all are dogs.
  My sister says dogs seldom bite,
But how can I be sure of this?
  Your sisters are not always right.

There is an awful dog I hear;
  It barks and barks as I go by.
I know some day it will get loose,
  And fiercely at my throat will fly.

And other dogs come round and sniff
  (I've sandals, and my legs are bare).
Perhaps it's true they will not bite;
  Perhaps some day I shall not care.

When you were five and walked to school,
  And you met things to tremble at,
Were you as brave as great big men,
  Or did your heart go pit-a-pat?

Ethel Turner

THE CLUCKING HEN

"Will you take a walk with me,
My little wife, to-day?
There's barley in the barley-field,
And hay-seed in the hay."

"Thank you," said the clucking hen;
"I've something else to do;
I'm busy sitting on my eggs,
I cannot walk with you."

"Cluck, cluck, cluck, cluck,"
Said the clucking hen;
"My little chicks will soon be hatched,
I'll think about it then."

Crack, crack, went all the eggs,
Out dropt the chickens small!
"Cluck!" said the clucking hen,
"Now I have you all.

"Come along, my little chicks,
I'll take a walk with YOU."
"Hullo!" said the barn-door cock,
"Cock-a-doodle-doo!"

Anne Hawkshaw

WHAT THE BIRDS SAY

Do you ask what the birds say
  The Sparrow, the Dove,
The Linnet and Thrush say,
  "I love and I love!"

In the winter they're silent–
  The wind is so strong;
What it says, I don't know,
  But it sings a loud song.

But green leaves, and blossoms,
  And sunny warm weather,
And singing and loving–
  All come back together.

But the lark is so brimful
  Of gladness and love,
The green fields below him,
  The blue sky above,

That he sings, and he sings;
  And for ever sings he–
'I love my Love,
  And my Love loves me!"

Samuel Taylor Coleridge

A SONG FROM THE SUDS

Queen of my tub, I merrily sing,
  While the white foam rises high;
And sturdily wash, and rinse, and wring,
  And fasten the clothes to dry;
Then out in the free fresh air they swing,
  Under the sunny sky.

"I wish we could wash from our hearts and souls
  The stains of the week away,
And let water and air by their magic make
  Ourselves as pure as they!
Then on the earth there would be indeed
  A glorious washing-day!

"Along the path of a useful life
  Will heart's-ease ever bloom;
The busy mind has no time to think
  Of sorrow, or care, or gloom;
And anxious thoughts may be swept away
  As we busily wield a broom.

"I am glad a task to me is given,
  To labour at day by day;
For it brings me health, and strength, and hope,
  And I cheerfully learn to say,
'Head, you may think, Heart, you may feel,
  But Hand, you shall work alway!' "

Louisa M. Alcott

GRASSHOPPER GREEN

Grasshopper Green is a comical chap;
  He lives on the best of fare.
Bright little trousers, jacket and cap,
  These are his summer wear.
Out in the meadow he loves to go,
  Playing away in the sun;
It's hopperty, skipperty, high and low,
  Summer's the time for fun.

Grasshopper Green has a quaint little house;
  It's under the hedge so gay.
Grandmother Spider, as still as a mouse,
  Watches him over the way.
Gladly he's calling the children, I know,
  Out in the beautiful sun;
It's hopperty, skipperty, high and low,
  Summer's the time for fun.

Anonymous

A JINGLE

A beetle got stuck in some jam,
And he cried, "How unhappy I am!"
  His Ma said, "Don't talk,
  If you really can't walk
You'd better go home in the tram!"

Jessie Pope

THE POND

There was a round pond, and a pretty pond too,
About it white daisies and violets grew,
And dark weeping willows, that stoop to the ground,
Dipped in their long branches, and shaded it round.

A party of ducks to this pond would repair,
To sport 'mid the green water-weeds that grew there:
Indeed, the assembly would frequently meet,
To discuss their affairs in this pleasant retreat.

Now the subjects on which they were wont to
converse,
I am sorry I cannot exactly rehearse;
For though I've oft listened in hopes of discerning
I own 'tis a matter that baffles my learning.

One day a young chicken that lived there-about,
Stood watching to see the ducks pop in and out,
Now turning tail upward, now diving below;
She thought, of all things, she should like to do so.

So the poor silly chick was determined to try;
She thought 'twas as easy to swim as to fly!
Though her mother had told her she must not go near,
She foolishly thought there was nothing to fear.

"My feet, wings, and feathers, for aught I can see,
Are as good as the ducks' are for swimming," said she:
" 'Though *my* beak is pointed, and *their* beaks are
round,
Is that any reason that I should be drowned?

"Why should I not swim, then, as well as a duck?
I think I shall venture, and e'en try my luck!
For," said she (spite of all that her mother had taught
her),
"I'm really remarkably fond of the water!"

So in this poor ignorant animal flew,
But soon found her dear mother's cautions were true:
She splashed, and she dashed, and she turned herself
round,
And heartily wished herself safe on the ground.

But now 'twas too late to begin to repent,
The harder she struggled the deeper she went;
And when every effort she vainly had tried,
She slowly sank down to the bottom and died!

The ducks, I perceived, began loudly to quack,
When they saw the poor fowl floating dead on its back;
And by their grave gestures and looks in dis-coursing,
Obedience to parents were plainly enforcing.

Jane and Ann Taylor

A CHINESE NURSERY-SONG

The mouse ran up the candlestick,
To eat the grease from off the wick.
When he got up, he could not get down,
But squeaked to waken all the town:
Ma-ma-ma! Ma-ma-ma!

From "Cradle Songs of Many Nations"

TIME TO RISE

A birdie with a yellow bill
Hopped upon the window sill,
Cocked his shining eye and said:
"Ain't you 'shamed, you sleepy head."

Robert Louis Stevenson

THE LAMB

Little lamb, who made thee?
Dost thou know who made thee?
Gave thee life, and bid thee feed
By the stream and o'er the mead;
Gave thee clothing of delight,
Softest clothing, woolly, bright;
Gave thee such a tender voice,
Making all the vales rejoice?
Little lamb, who made thee?
Dost thou know who made thee?

Little lamb, I'll tell thee,
Little lamb, I'll tell thee:
He is called by thy name,
For he calls himself a lamb.
He is meek, and he is mild;
He became a little child.
I a child, and thou a lamb,
We are called by his name.
Little lamb, God bless thee!
Little lamb, God bless thee!

William Blake

A VISIT FROM ST. NICHOLAS

'Twas the night before Christmas, when all through
  the house
Not a creature was stirring, not even a mouse;
The stockings were hung by the chimney with care,
In hopes that St. Nicholas soon would be there;
The children were nestled all snug in their beds,
While visions of sugar-plums danced in their heads;
And mamma in her 'kerchief, and I in my cap,
Had just settled our brains for a long winter's nap–
When out on the lawn there arose such a clatter,
I sprang from my bed to see what was the matter.
Away to the window I flew like a flash,
Tore open the shutters, and threw up the sash.
The moon, on the breast of the new-fallen snow,
Gave the lustre of midday to objects below;
When, what to my wondering eyes should appear,
But a miniature sleigh and eight tiny reindeer,
With a little old driver, so lively and quick,
I knew in a moment it must be St. Nick.
More rapid than eagles his coursers they came,
And he whistled, and shouted, and called them
  by name:
'Now, *Dasher*! now, *Dancer!* now, *Prancer* and *Vixen!*
On, *Comet*! on, *Cupid*! on, *Donder* and *Blitzen*!

To the top of the porch! to the top of the wall!
Now dash away! dash away! dash away all!'
As dry leaves that before the wild hurricane fly,
When they meet with an obstacle, mount to the sky;
So up to the house-top the coursers they flew
With the sleigh full of toys, and St. Nicholas too.
And then, in a twinkling, I heard on the roof
The prancing and pawing of each little hoof–
As I drew in my head, and was turning around,
Down the chimney St. Nicholas came with a bound.
He was dressed all in fur, from his head to his foot,
And his clothes were all tarnished with ashes and soot;
A bundle of toys he had flung on his back,
And he looked like a pedlar just opening his pack.
His eyes–how they twinkled; his dimples, how merry!
His cheeks were like roses, his nose like a cherry!
His droll little mouth was drawn up like a bow,
And the beard of his chin was as white as the snow;
The stump of a pipe he held tight in his teeth,
And the smoke it encircled his head like a wreath;
He had a broad face and a little round belly
That shook, when he laughed, like a bowl full of jelly.
He was chubby and plump, a right jolly old elf,
And I laughed when I saw him, in spite of myself;
A wink of his eye and a twist of his head
Soon gave me to know I had nothing to dread;

continued on next page

He spoke not a word, but went straight to his work,
And filled all the stockings; then turned with a jerk,
And laying his finger aside of his nose,
And giving a nod, up the chimney he rose;
He sprang to his sleigh, to his team gave a whistle,
And away they all flew like the down of a thistle.
But I heard him exclaim, ere he drove out of sight,
'Happy Christmas to all, and to all a good night!'

Clement Clarke Moore

DAYS OF BIRTH

Monday's child is fair of face,
Tuesday's child is full of grace,
Wednesday's child is full of woe,
Thursday's child has far to go,

Friday's child is loving and giving,
Saturday's child works hard for its living,
But the child that is born on the Sabbath Day
Is bonny, and blithe, and good, and gay.

Old Rhyme

DAYS OF BIRTH

CLEAN CLARA

CLEAN CLARA

What! not know our Clean Clara?
Why, the hot folks in Sahara,
And the cold Esquimaux,
Our little Clara know!
Clean Clara, the poet sings,
Cleaned a hundred thousand things!

She cleaned the keys of the harpsicord,
She cleaned the hilt of the family sword,
She cleaned my lady, she cleaned my lord;
All the pictures in their frames,
Knights with daggers, and stomachered dames–
Cecils, Godfreys, Montforts, Græmes,
Winifreds–all those nice old names!

She cleaned the works of the eight-day clock,
She cleaned the spring of a secret lock;
She cleaned the mirror, she cleaned the cupboard;
All the books she India-rubbered!
She cleaned the Dutch-tiles in the place,
She cleaned some very old-fashioned lace;
The Countess of Miniver came to her,
"Pray, my dear, will you clean my fur?"

continued on next page

All her cleanings are admirable;
To count your teeth you will be able,
If you look in the walnut-table!

She cleaned the tent-stitch and the sampler;
She cleaned the tapestry, which was ampler;
She cleaned the drops of the chandeliers,
Madam in mittens was moved to tears!

She cleaned the cage of the cockatoo,
The oldest bird that ever grew;
I should say a thousand years would do–
I'm sure he looked it, but nobody knew;
She cleaned the china, she cleaned the delft;
She cleaned the baby, she cleaned herself!

To-morrow morning she means to try
To clean the cobwebs from the sky;
Some people say the girl will rue it,
But my belief is she will do it.

So I've made up my mind to be there to see,
There's a beautiful place in the walnut-tree,
The bough is as firm as the solid rock;
She brings out her broom at six o'clock.

William Brighty Rands

OUR VISIT TO THE ZOO

When we went to the Zoo
We saw a gnu,
An elk and a whelk
And a wild emu.

We saw a hare,
And a bear in his lair,
And a seal have a meal
On a high-backed chair.

We saw a snake
That was hardly awake,
And a lion eat meat
They'd forgotten to bake.

We saw a coon
And a baby baboon.
The giraffe made us laugh
All afternoon!

We saw a crab and a long-tailed dab,
And we all went home in a taxi-cab.

Jessie Pope

THE PIED PIPER OF HAMELIN

Hamelin Town's in Brunswick,
  By famous Hanover city;
The river Weser, deep and wide,
Washes its wall on the southern side;
A pleasanter spot you never spied;
  But, when begins my ditty,
Almost five hundred years ago,
To see the townsfolk suffer so
  From vermin, was a pity.

  Rats!
They fought the dogs and killed the cats,
  And bit the babies in the cradles,
And ate the cheeses out of the vats,
  And licked the soup from the cooks' own ladles,
Split open the kegs of salted sprats,
Made nests inside men's Sunday hats,
And even spoiled the women's chats
  By drowning their speaking
  With shrieking and squeaking
In fifty different sharps and flats.

At last the people in a body
  To the Town Hall came flocking:

‘ ’Tis clear,’ cried they, ‘our Mayor’s a noddy;
  And as for our Corporation–shocking
To think we buy gowns lined with ermine
For dolts that can’t or won’t determine
What’s best to rid us of our vermin!
You hope, because you’re old and obese,
To find in the furry civic robe ease?
Rouse up, sirs! Give your brains a racking
To find the remedy we’re lacking,
Or, sure as fate, we’ll send you packing!’
At this the Mayor and Corporation
Quaked with a mighty consternation.

An hour they sat in council,
  At length the Mayor broke silence:
‘For a guilder I’d my ermine gown sell,
  I wish I were a mile hence!
It’s easy to bid one rack one’s brain–
I’m sure my poor head aches again,
I’ve scratched it so, and all in vain.
Oh for a trap, a trap, a trap!’
Just as he said this, what should hap
At the chamber door but a gentle tap?
‘Bless us,’ cried the Mayor, ‘what’s that?’
(With the Corporation as he sat,
Looking little though wondrous fat;
Nor brighter was his eye, nor moister
Than a too-long-opened oyster,

continued on next page

Save when at noon his paunch grew mutinous
For a plate of turtle, green and glutinous)
'Only a scraping of shoes on the mat?
Anything like the sound of a rat
Makes my heart go pit-a-pat!'

'Come in!' the Mayor cried, looking bigger:
And in did come the strangest figure!
His queer long coat from heel to head
Was half of yellow and half of red,
And he himself was tall and thin,
With sharp blue eyes, each like a pin,
And light loose hair, yet swarthy skin,
No tuft on cheek nor beard on chin,
But lips where smiles went out and in;
There was no guessing his kith and kin:
And nobody could enough admire
The tall man and his quaint attire.
Quoth one: 'It's as my great-grandsire,
Starting up at the Trump of Doom's tone,
Had walked this way from his painted tombstone!'

He advanced to the council-table:
And, 'Please your honours,' said he, 'I'm able,
By means of a secret charm, to draw
  All creatures living beneath the sun,
  That creep or swim or fly or run,
After me so as you never saw!

And I chiefly use my charm
On creatures that do people harm,
The mole and toad and newt and viper;
And people call me the Pied Piper.'
(And here they noticed round his neck
  A scarf of red and yellow stripe,
To match with his coat of the self-same check;
  And at the scarf's end hung a pipe;
And his fingers, they noticed, were ever straying
As if impatient to be playing
Upon this pipe, as low it dangled
Over his vesture, so old-fangled.)
'Yet,' said he, 'poor piper as I am,
In Tartary I freed the Cham,
  Last June, from his huge swarms of gnats;
I eased in Asia the Nizam
  Of a monstrous brood of vampire-bats:
And as for what your brain bewilders,
  If I can rid your town of rats
Will you give me a thousand guilders?'
'One? fifty thousand!'–was the exclamation
Of the astonished Mayor and Corporation.

Into the street the Piper stept,
  Smiling first a little smile,
As if he knew what magic slept
  In his quiet pipe the while;
Then, like a musical adept,

continued on next page

To blow the pipe his lips he wrinked,
And green and blue his sharp eyes twinkled,
Like a candle-flame where salt is sprinkled;
And ere three shrill notes the pipe uttered,
You heard as if an army muttered;
And the muttering grew to a grumbling;
And the grumbling grew to a mighty rumbling;
And out of the houses the rats came tumbling.
Great rats, small rats, lean rats, brawny rats,
Brown rats, black rats, grey rats, tawny rats,
Grave old plodders, gay young friskers,
   Fathers, mothers, uncles, cousins,
Cocking tails and pricking whiskers,
   Families by tens and dozens,
Brothers, sisters, husbands, wives–
Followed the Piper for their lives.
From street to street he piped advancing,
And step for step they followed dancing,
Until they came to the river Weser,
   Wherein all plunged and perished!
–Save one who, stout as Julius Caesar,
Swam across and lived to carry
   (As he, the manuscript he cherished)
To Rat-land home his commentary:
Which was, 'At the first shrill notes of the pipe,
I heard a sound as of scraping tripe,
And putting apples, wondrous ripe,
Into a cider-press's gripe:

And a moving away of pickle-tub-boards,
And a leaving ajar of conserve-cupboards,
And a drawing the corks of train-oil-flasks,
And a breaking the hoops of butter-casks;
And it seemed as if a voice
  (Sweeter far than by harp or by psaltery
Is breathed) called out, "Oh rats, rejoice!
  The world is grown to one vast drysaltery!
So munch on, crunch on, take your nuncheon,
Breakfast, supper, dinner, luncheon!"
And just as a bulky sugar-puncheon,
All ready staved, like a great sun shone
Glorious scarce an inch before me,
Just as methought it said, "Come, bore me!"
–I found the Weser rolling o'er me.'

You should have heard the Hamelin people
Ringing the bells till they rocked the steeple.
'Go,' cried the Mayor, 'and get long poles,
Poke out the nests and block up the holes!
Consult with carpenters and builders,
And leave in our town not even a trace
Of the rats!'–when suddenly, up the face
Of the Piper perked in the market-place,
With a 'First, if you please, my thousand guilders!'

A thousand guilders! The Mayor looked blue;
So did the Corporation too.

continued on next page

For council dinners made rare havoc
With Claret, Moselle, Vin-de-Grave, Hock;
And half the money would replenish
Their cellar's biggest butt with Rhenish.
To pay this sum to a wandering fellow
With a gipsy coat of red and yellow!
'Beside,' quoth the Mayor with a knowing wink,
'Our business was done at the river's brink;
We saw with our eyes the vermin sink,
And what's dead can't come to life, I think.
So, friend, we're not the folks to shrink
From the duty of giving you something for drink,
And a matter of money to put in your poke;
But as for the guilders, what we spoke
Of them, as you very well know, was in joke.
Besides, our losses have made us thrifty.
A thousand guilders! Come, take fifty!'

The Piper's face fell, and he cried
'No trifling! I can't wait, beside!
I've promised to visit by dinnertime
Baghdad, and accept the prime
Of the Head-Cook's pottage, all he's rich in,
For having left, in the Caliph's kitchen,
Of a nest of scorpions no survivor:
With him I proved no bargain-driver,
With you, don't think I'll bate a stiver!
And folks who put me in a passion
May find me pipe after another fashion.'

'How?' cried the Mayor, 'd'ye think I brook
Being worse treated than a cook?
Insulted by a lazy ribald
With idle pipe and vesture piebald?
You threaten us, fellow? Do your worst,
Blow your pipe there till you burst!'

Once more he stepped into the street
  And to his lips again
  Laid his long pipe of smooth straight cane;
And ere he blew three notes (such sweet
Soft notes as yet musician's cunning
  Never gave the enraptured air)
There was a rustling that seemed like a bustling
Of merry crowds justling at pitching and hustling
Small feet were pattering, wooden shoes clattering,
Little hands clapping and little tongues chattering,
And, like fowls in a farmyard
  when barley is scattering,
Out came the children running.
All the little boys and girls,
With rosy cheeks and flaxen curls,
And sparkling eyes and teeth like pearls,
Tripping and skipping, ran merrily after
The wonderful music with shouting and laughter.

The Mayor was dumb, and the Council stood
As if they were changed into blocks of wood,

continued on next page

Unable to move a step, or cry
To the children merrily skipping by
–Could only follow with the eye
That joyous crowd at the Piper's back.
But how the Mayor was on the rack,
And the wretched Council's bosoms beat,
As the Piper turned from the High Street
To where the Weser rolled its waters
Right in the way of their sons and daughters!
However he turned from south to west,
And to Koppelberg Hill his steps addressed,
And after him the children pressed;
Great was the joy in every breast.
'He never can cross that mighty top!
He's forced to let the piping drop,
And we shall see our children stop!'
When, lo, as they reached the mountain-side,
A wondrous portal opened wide,
As if a cavern was suddenly hollowed;
And the Piper advanced and the children followed,
And when all were in to the very last,
The door in the mountain-side shut fast.
Did I say, all? No! One was lame,
  And could not dance the whole of the way;
And in after years, if you would blame
  His sadness, he was used to say–
'It's dull in our town since my playmates left!
I can't forget that I'm bereft

Of all the pleasant sights they see,
Which the Piper also promised me.
For he led us, he said, to a joyous land,
Joining the town and just at hand,
Where waters gushed and fruit trees grew
And flowers put forth a fairer hue,
And everything was strange and new;
The sparrows were brighter than peacocks here,
And their dogs outran our fallow deer,
And honey-bees had lost their stings,
And horses were born with eagles' wings:
And just as I became assured
My lame foot would be speedily cured,
The music stopped and I stood still,
And found myself outside the hill,
Left alone against my will,
To go now limping as before,
And never hear of that country more!'

Alas, alas for Hamelin!
  There came into many a burgher's pate
  A text which says that heaven's gate
  Opes to the rich at as easy rate
As the needle's eye takes a camel in!
The Mayor sent east, west, north, and south,
To offer the Piper, by word of mouth,
  Wherever it was men's lot to find him,

continued on next page

Silver and gold to his heart's content,
If he'd only return the way he went,
   And bring the children behind him.
But when they saw 'twas a lost endeavour,
And Piper and dancers were gone for ever,
They made a decree that lawyers never
   Should think their records dated duly
If, after the day of the month and year,
These words did not as well appear,
'And so long after what happened here
   On the Twenty-second of July,
Thirteen hundred and seventy-six':
And the better in memory to fix
The place of the children's last retreat,
They called it the Pied Piper's Street–
Where anyone playing on pipe or tabor
Was sure for the future to lose his labour.
Nor suffered they hostelry or tavern
   To shock with mirth a street so solemn;
But opposite the place of the cavern
   They wrote the story on a column;
And on the great church-window painted
The same, to make the world acquainted
How their children were stolen away,
And their it stands to this very day.

And I must not omit to say
That in Transylvania there's a tribe
Of alien people who ascribe

The outlandish ways and dress
On which their neighbours lay such stress,
To their fathers and mothers having risen
Out of some subterraneous prison
Into which they were trepanned
Long time ago in a mighty band
Out of Hamelin town in Brunswick land,
But how or why, they don't understand.

So, Willy, let you and me be wipers
Of scores out with all men–especially pipers!
And, whether they pipe us free from rats or from mice,
If we've promised them aught, let us keep our
promise!

Robert Browning

THE LAND OF COUNTERPANE

When I was sick and lay a-bed,
I had two pillows at my head,
And all my toys beside me lay
To keep me happy all the day.

And sometimes for an hour or so
I watched my leaden soldiers go,
With different uniforms and drills,
Among the bed-clothes, through the hills;

And sometimes sent my ships in fleets
All up and down among the sheets;
Or brought my trees and houses out,
And planted cities all about.

I was the giant great and still
That sits upon the pillow-hill,
And sees before him, dale and plain,
The pleasant land of counterpane.

Robert Louis Stevenson

LAND OF COUNTERPANE

WYNKEN, BLYNKEN, AND NOD

WYNKEN, BLYNKEN, AND NOD

Wynken, Blynken, and Nod one night
  Sailed off in a wooden shoe,–
Sailed on a river of crystal light
  Into a sea of dew.
"Where are you going, and what do you wish?"
  Thc old moon asked the three.
"We have come to fish for the herring-fish
  That live in this beautiful sea;
Nets of silver and gold have we,"

Said Wynken,
Blynken,
And Nod.

The old moon laughed and sang a song,
  As they rocked in the wooden shoe;
And the wind that sped them all night long
  Ruffled the waves of dew.
The little stars were the herring-fish
  That lived in the beautiful sea–
"Now cast your nets wherever you wish,
  Never afeared are we!"
So cried the stars to the fishermen three:

continued on next page

Wynken,
Blynken,
And Nod.

All night long their nets they threw
For the fish in the twinkling foam,
Then down from the sky came the wooden shoe,
Bringing the fishermen home;
'Twas all so pretty a sail, it seemed
As if it could not be;
And some folk thought 'twas a dream they'd dreamed
Of sailing that beautiful sea–
But I shall name you the fishermen three:

Wynken,
Blynken,
And Nod.

Wynken and Blynken are two little eyes,
And Nod is a little head,
And the wooden shoe that sailed the skies
Is a wee one's trundle-bed;
So shut your eyes while Mother sings
Of wonderful sights that be,
And you shall see the beautiful things,
As you rock in the misty sea,
Where the old shoe rocked the fishermen three–
Wynken, Blynken, and Nod.

Eugene Field

CRADLE SONG

What does little birdie say
In her nest at peep of day?
Let me fly, says little birdie,
Mother, let me fly away.
Birdie, rest a little longer,
Till the little wings are stronger.
So she rests a little longer,
Then she flies away.

What does little baby say,
In her bed at peep of day?
Baby says, like little birdie,
Let me rise and fly away.
Baby, sleep a little longer,
Till the little limbs are stronger.
If she sleeps a little longer,
Baby too shall fly away.

Alfred, Lord Tennyson

THE BAD BOY

Once a little round-eyed lad
Determined to be very bad.

He called his porridge nasty pap,
And threw it all in nurse's lap.

His gentle sister's cheek he hurt,
He smudged his pinny in the dirt.

He found the bellows, and he blew
The pet canary right in two!

And when he went to bed at night
He would not say his prayers aright.

This pained a lovely twinkling star
That watched the trouble from afar.

She told her bright-faced friends, and soon
The dreadful rumour reached the moon.

The moon, a gossiping old dame,
Told Father Sun the bad boy's shame.

And then the giant sun began
A very satisfactory plan.

Upon the naughty rebel's face
He would not pour his beamy grace.

The little garden of the boy
Seemed desert, missing heaven's joy.

He also lost, by his disgrace,
That indoor's sun, his mother's face.

His father sent him up to bed
With neither kiss nor pat for head.

O little boys, who would not miss
A father's and a mother's kiss,

Who would not cause a sister pain,
Who want the sun to shine again,

Who want sweet beams to tend the plot
Where grows the pet forget-me-not,

Who hate a life of streaming eyes,
Be good, be merry, and be wise.

Norman Gale

THE MAD GARDENER'S SONG

He thought he saw an Elephant,
That practised on a fife:
He looked again, and found it was
A letter from his wife.
'At length I realise,' he said,
'The bitterness of Life!'

He thought he saw a Buffalo
Upon the chimney-piece:
He looked again, and found it was
His Sister's Husband's Niece.
'Unless you leave this house,' he said,
I'll send for the Police!'

He thought he saw a Rattlesnake
That questioned him in Greek:
He looked again, and found it was
The Middle of Next Week.
'The one thing I regret,' he said,
'Is that it cannot speak!'

He thought he saw a Banker's Clerk
Descending from the bus:
He looked again, and found it was
A Hippopotamus:
'If this should stay to dine,' he said,
'There won't be much for us!'

He thought he saw a Kangaroo
  That worked a coffee-mill:
He looked again, and found it was
  A Vegetable-Pill.
'Were I to swallow this,' he said,
  'I should be very ill!'

He thought he saw a Coach-and-Four
  That stood beside his bed:
He looked again, and found it was
  A Bear without a Head.
'Poor thing,' he said, 'poor silly thing!
  It's waiting to be fed!'

He thought he saw an Albatross
  That fluttered round the lamp:
He looked again, and found it was
  A Penny-Postage-Stamp.
'You'd best be getting home,' he said:
  'The nights are very damp!'

He thought he saw an Argument
  That proved he was the Pope:
He looked again, and found it was
  A Bar of Mottled Soap.
'A fact so dread,' he faintly said,
'Extinguishes all hope!'

Lewis Carroll

WHAT IS PINK

What is pink? A rose is pink
By the fountain's brink.
What is red? A poppy's red
In its barley bed.
What is blue? The sky is blue
Where the clouds float through.
What is white? A swan is white
Sailing in the light.
What is yellow? Pears are yellow,
Rich and ripe and mellow.
What is green? The grass is green,
With small flowers between.
What is violet? Clouds are violet
In the summer twilight.
What is orange? Why, an orange,
Just an orange!

Christina Rossetti

THE MOUNTAIN AND THE SQUIRREL

The mountain and the squirrel
Had a quarrel,
And the former called the latter "Little prig";
Bun replied,
"You are doubtless very big;
But all sorts of things and weather
Must be taken in together
To make up a year,
And a sphere.
And I think it no disgrace
To occupy my place–
If I'm not so large as you,
You are not so small as I,
And not half so spry:
I'll not deny you make
A very pretty squirrel track.
Talents differ; all is well and wisely put;
If I cannot carry forests on my back,
Neither can you crack a nut."

Ralph Waldo Emerson

THE CHRISTMAS TURKEY

"Obble, obble," said the Turkey as he strutted up
and down,
"I really am the finest bird in all the country town.
How full my breast, how large my legs, my comb
how red and gay,
I'm sure to be a bonny bird by merry Christmas day,
Oh, won't I obble happily on jolly Christmas day!"

"Quack, quack," went all the ducklings as they
wobbled to the stream,
"We wish we were all Turkeys; isn't he a perfect
dream?"
"Cluck, cluck," the young hen shouted, "Come, my
chicks, out of his way
Or you won't see how big the Turkey is on Christmas
day,
A sight I'm looking forward to on jolly Christmas
day."

"Bow wow," remarked the house-dog old to Tabby
at the door,
"Bow wow, we've seen the turkeys grow as fat and
fine before."

"Oh yes, meow, meow," said Tabby, who now is
going grey,
"They have a trick of getting fat until it's Christmas
day–
But they get no fatter, do they, after jolly Christmas
day?"

When Christmas came I heard the ducklings quack
and saw them wobble,
But no one saw the Turkey strut and no one heard
him obble.
They asked the house-dog and the cat, who said,
"He's gone away
To cheer the hungry company who meet on Christmas
day,
Who love to meet fat turkeys on a jolly Christmas
day."

"Bow wow, it was too cold for him in this bleak
farmyard spot;"
"Meow, meow, and so they took him in and made
him nice and hot."
"So now, you hens and chickens, and you ducklings,
run and play,
And give thanks you are not Turkeys who grow fat
till Christmas day,
But who never obble happily on jolly Christmas day."

L. Elise

BEDTIME IN SUMMER

In winter it is often dark
  Before we have our tea,
But in the summer it's quite light
  When Bedtime comes for me.

The sky is still quite blue and clear,
  The flow'rs are wide awake,
And only I among them all
  My way to bed must take.

The little stream runs gaily by,
  The soft wind shakes the tree,
The roses to each other nod,
  As tho' they laugh'd at me.

But never mind, for tho' just now
  To sleep by day seems wrong,
The roses when *they* go to bed
  Stay there all winter long.

Augusta Hancock

LULLABY OF AN INFANT CHIEF

Oh, hush thee, my babie, thy sire was a knight,
Thy mother a lady, both lovely and bright;
The woods and the glens, from the towers which we
  see,
They all are belonging, dear babie, to thee.

Oh, fear not the bugle, though loudly it blows,
It calls but the warders that guard thy repose;
Their bows would be bended, their blades would be
  red,
Ere the step of a foeman drew near to thy bed.

Oh, hush thee, my babie, the time soon will come,
When thy sleep shall be broken by trumpet and drum;
Then hush thee, my darling, take rest while you may,
For strike comes with manhood, and waking with day.

Sir Walter Scott

THE LITTLE FISH THAT WOULD NOT DO AS IT WAS BID

"Dear mother," said a little fish,
"Pray is not that a fly?
I'm very hungry, and I wish
You'd let me go and try."

"Sweet innocent," the mother cried,
And started from her nook,
"That horrid fly is put to hide
The sharpness of the hook."

Now, as I've heard, this little trout
Was young and foolish too,
And so he thought he'd venture out,
To see if it were true.

And round about the hook he played,
With many a longing look,
And–"Dear me," to himself he said,
"I'm sure that's not a hook.

"I can but give one little pluck:
Let's see, and so I will."
So on he went, and lo! it stuck
Quite through his little gill.

And as he faint and fainter grew,
With hollow voice he cried,
"Dear mother, had I minded you
I need not now have died."

Jane and Ann Taylor

SWEET AND LOW

Sweet and low, sweet and low,
Wind of the western sea,
Low, low, breathe and blow,
Wind of the western sea!
Over the rolling waters go,
Come from the dying moon, and blow,
Blow him again to me;
While my little one, while my pretty one, sleeps.

Sleep and rest, sleep and rest,
Father will come to thee soon;
Rest, rest, on mother's breast,
Father will come to thee soon;
Father will come to his babe in the nest,
Silver sails all out of the west
Under the silver moon:
Sleep, my little one, sleep, my pretty one, sleep.

Alfred, Lord Tennyson

CHILDREN'S MAY SONG

Spring is coming, spring is coming,
  Birdies, build your nest;
Weave together straw and feather,
  Doing each your best.

Spring is coming, spring is coming,
  Flowers are coming too:
Pansies, lilies, daffodillies
  Now are coming through.

Spring is coming, spring is coming,
  All around is fair:
Shimmer and quiver on the river,
  Joy is everywhere.

We wish you a happy May.

Traditional

CHILDREN'S MAY SONG

THE OLD MAN IN THE MOON

THE OLD MAN IN THE MOON

"Say, where have you been, Frank–say,
where have you been?"
"Oh! I've been a long way: I've been to
the moon."
"But how did you get there? and what have
you seen?"
"Oh! I went, to be sure, in my little balloon.

"And I've seen–why, I've seen the old man
who lives there;
And his mouth, it grew bigger the nearer I
got;
So I pulled off my hat, made a bow with an
air,
And said, 'Sir, you inhabit a very bright
spot.'

"And the old man he laughed, he laughed long
and loud;
And he patted my cheek as he graciously
said,
'You had better return, nor get lost in a
cloud;
And besides, it is time that we both were in
bed.' "

Old Rhyme

MR. FLY

What a sharp little fellow is Mister Fly!
He goes where he pleases, low or high,
And can walk just as well with his feet to the sky
  As I can on the floor.
    At the window he comes
  With a buzz and a roar,
    And o'er the smooth glass
    Can easily pass
  Or through the keyhole of the door.
He eats the sugar and goes away,
Nor ever once asks what there is to pay;
And sometimes he crosses the teapot's steam,
And comes and plunges his head in the cream;
Then on the edge of the jug he stands,
And cleans his wings with his feet and hands.

This done, through the window he hurries away,
And gives a buzz, as if to say,
"At present I haven't a minute to stay,
But I'll peep in again in the course of the day."
    Then away he'll fly,
    Where the sunbeams lie,
    And neither stop to shake hands,
    Nor bid one good-bye.

Such a strange little fellow is Mister Fly,
Who goes where he pleases, low or high,
    And can walk on the ceiling
    Without ever feeling
A fear of tumbling down "sky high!"

Thomas Miller

MUSTARD AND CRESS

Elizabeth, my cousin, is the sweetest little girl,
From her eyes like dark blue pansies to her tiniest golden curl;
I do not use her great long name, but simply call her Bess,
And yesterday I planted her in mustard and in cress.

My garden is so narrow that there's very little room,
But I'd rather have her name than get a holly-hock to bloom;
And before she comes to visit us, with Charley and with Jess,
She'll pop up green and bonny out of mustard and of cress.

Norman Gale

THE LITTLE RAIN-DROPS

Oh! where do you come from,
  You little drops of rain;
Pitter-patter, pitter-patter,
  Down the window pane?

They won't let me walk
  And they won't let me play,
And they won't let me go
  Out of doors at all to-day.

They put away my playthings
  Because I broke them all;
And then they locked up all my bricks,
  And took away my ball.

Tell me, little rain-drops,
  Is that the way you play,
Pitter-patter, pitter-patter,
  All the rainy day?

They say I'm very naughty,
  Yet I've nothing else to do
But sit here at the window;
  I should like to play with you.

The little rain-drops cannot speak,
  But "pitter-patter-pat"
Means: "We can play on *this* side,
  Why can't you play on *that*?"

Anne Hawkshaw

YELLOW CHICKS

Yellow chicks, the baby things,
  Bits of fluff and feather;
Underneath their mother's wings,
  Cuddled up together!
Never mind the wind and rain;
  Cold or any other,
Everything is bright again,
  Cuddled up to mother!

Florence Hoatson

A GRACE

Some hae meat, and canna eat,
And some wad eat that want it;
But we hae meat and we can eat,
And sae the Lord be thankit.

Robert Burns

THE HUMP

The Camel's hump is an ugly lump
  Which well you may see at the Zoo;
But uglier yet is the hump we get
  From having too little to do.

Kiddies and grown-ups too-oo-oo,
If we haven't enough to do-oo-oo,
    We get the hump–
    Cameelious hump–
The hump that is black and blue!

We climb out of bed with a frouzly head,
  And a snarly-yarly voice.
We shiver and scowl and we grunt and we growl
  At our bath and our boots and our toys;

And there ought to be a corner for me
(And I know there is one for you)
    When we get the hump–
    Cameelious hump–
The hump that is black and blue!

The cure for this ill is not to sit still,
  Or frowst with a book by the fire;
But to take a large hoe and a shovel also,
  And dig till you gently perspire;

And then you will find that the sun and the wind,
And the Djinn of the Garden too,
    Have lifted the hump–
    The horrible hump–
The hump that is black and blue!

I get it as well as you-oo-oo–
If I haven't enough to do-oo-oo!
    We all get hump–
    Cameelious hump–
Kiddies and grown-ups too!

Rudyard Kipling

THE FIRST OF MAY

The fair maid who, the First of May,
  Goes to the fields at break of day,
And washes in dew from the hawthorn tree,
  Will ever after handsome be.

Traditional

THE SUGAR-PLUM TREE

Have you ever heard of the Sugar-Plum Tree?
'Tis a marvel of great renown!
It blooms on the shore of the Lollipop Sea
In the garden of Shut-Eye Town;
The fruit it bears is so wondrously sweet
(As those who have tasted it say)
That good little children have only to eat
Of that fruit to be happy next day.

When you've got to the tree, you would have a hard time
To capture the fruit which I sing;
The tree is so tall that no person could climb
To the boughs where the sugar-plums swing!
But up in that tree sits a chocolate cat,
And a gingerbread dog prowls below;
And this is the way you contrive to get at
Those sugar-plums tempting you so:

You say but the word to that gingerbread dog,
And he barks with such terrible zest
That the chocolate cat is at once all agog,
As her swelling proportions attest.

And the chocolate cat goes cavorting around
From *this* leafy limb unto *that,*
And the sugar-plums tumble, of course, to the ground,–
Hurrah for that chocolate cat!

There are marshmallows, gum-drops and peppermint canes,
With stripings of scarlet or gold,
And you carry away of the treasure that rains
As much as your apron can hold!
So come, little child, cuddle closer to me
In your dainty white nightcap and gown,
And I'll rock you away to that Sugar-Plum Tree
In the garden of Shut-Eye Town.

Eugene Field

TO SANTA CLAUS UP THE CHIMNEY

Dear Santa Claus, you live, they say,
In Fairyland so far away,
But up the chimney you can hear
As well as if you stood quite near;
So listen now to my request–
You whom I love the very best–
For since the faery world began,
From Puck to darling Peter Pan,
Of all the fairies old and new,
There's no one, Santa, *just* like you!
Please put my name upon your list
Of children who must *not* be missed
When in your reindeer sledge you leave
The Land of Toys on Christmas Eve,
And in our waiting stocking pour
All kinds of wonders from your store.
I'll go to bed so soon that night
And let them take away the light,
And shut my eyes and fall asleep,
And never meanly try to peep;
And oh, if this is any guide,
Our kitchen chimney's extra wide,
And Daddy's stocking you will see
Hung up, instead of mine, for me!

Well, first I'd like down in the toe,
If you'll excuse my saying so,
A piece of money, bright and new
(Of course the size I leave to you);
And in the foot and leg you could
Pack heaps of treasures if you would:
A Noah's Ark in red and green,
A picture book, some plasticine,
And p'raps, if you have one to spare,
A lovely woolly Teddy Bear;
And then, dear Santa, *do* you think
A lady-doll, in blue or pink,
Right at the stocking-top might be
With arms of wax stretched out to me,
And say "Mamma" when I just press
A button underneath her dress?

But oh, dear me, was ever such
A greedy girl to want so much,
When crowds of eager children call
Your magic name up chimneys tall?
If I don't stop, there's not a doubt
Some one will have to go without,
So as you'll know what's best to do,
I leave the business all to you;

continued on next page

But if some child that's sad or poor
Wants what I've asked for, please be *sure*
You fill that stocking first, and see
There's only what is left for me,
And now good-bye, dear Santa Claus,
I love you *very* much, because
You're good and kind, and always care
For little children everywhere;
And when at last on Christmas Day
You've made so many glad and gay,
We'll not forget to wish that YOU
May have a Merry Christmas too!

Mary Farrah

AUTUMN FIRES

In the other gardens
  And all up the vale,
From the autumn bonfires
  See the smoke trail!

Pleasant summer over
  And all the summer flowers,
The red fire blazes,
  The grey smoke towers.

Sing a song of seasons!
  Something bright in all!
Flowers in the summer,
  Fires in the fall!

Robert Louis Stevenson

THE WORLD'S MUSIC

The world's a very happy place,
  Where every child should dance and sing,
And always have a smiling face,
  And never sulk for anything.

I waken when the morning's come,
  And feel the air and light alive
With strange sweet music, like the hum
  Of bees about their busy hive.

The linnets play among the leaves
  At hide-and-seek, and chirp and sing;
While, flashing to and from the eaves,
  The swallows twitter on the wing.

And twigs that shake, and boughs that sway;
  And tall old trees you could not climb;
And winds that come, but cannot stay,
  Are singing gaily all the time.

From dawn to dark the old mill-wheel
  Makes music, going round and round;
And dusty-white with flour and meal,
  The miller whistles to its sound.

The brook that flows beside the mill,
  As happy as a brook can be,
Goes singing its own song until
  It learns the singing of the sea.

For every wave upon the sands
  Sings songs you never tire to hear,
Of laden ships from sunny lands
  Where it is summer all the year.

And if you listen to the rain
  When leaves and birds and bees are dumb,
You hear it pattering on the pane
  Like Andrew beating on his drum.

The world is such a happy place
  That children, whether big or small,
Should always have a smiling face,
  And never, never sulk at all.

Gabriel Setoun

THE PEDLAR'S CARAVAN

I wish I lived in a caravan,
With a horse to drive, like a pedlar-man!
Where he comes from nobody knows,
Or where he goes to, but on he goes!

His caravan has windows two,
And a chimney of tin, that the smoke comes through;
He has a wife with a baby brown,
And they go a-riding from town to town.

Chairs to mend, and delft to sell!
He clashes the basins like a bell;
Tea-trays, baskets ranged in order,
Plates, with alphabets round the border!

The roads are brown, and the sea is green,
But his house is like a bathing-machine;
The world is round, and he can ride,
Rumble and splash, to the other side!

With the pedlar-man I should like to roam,
And write a book when I came home;
All the people would read my book,
Just like the Travels of Captain Cook!

William Brighty Rands

THE PEDLAR'S CARAVAN

ONCE I SAW A LITTLE BOAT

ONCE I SAW A LITTLE BOAT

Once I saw a little boat, and a pretty, pretty boat,
When daybreak the hills was adorning,
And into it I jumped, and away I did float,
So very, very early in the morning.

For every little wave has its nightcap on,
Its nightcap, white cap, nightcap on,
For every little wave has its nightcap on,
So very, very early in the morning.

All the fishes were asleep in their caves cool and deep,
When the ripple round my keel flashed a warning;
Said the minnow to the skate, "We must certainly be late,
Though I thought 'twas very early in the morning."

For every little wave has its nightcap on,
Its nightcap, white cap, nightcap on,
For every little wave has its nightcap on,
So very, very early in the morning.

continued on next page

The lobster, darkly green, soon appeared upon the
scene,
And pearly drops his claws were adorning;
Quoth he, "May I be boiled, if I'll have my pleasure
spoiled
So very, very early in the morning!

For every little wave has its nightcap on,
Its nightcap, white cap, nightcap on,
For every little wave has its nightcap on,
So very, very early in the morning.

Said the sturgeon to the eel, "Just imagine how I feel,
Thus roused without a syllable of warning;
People ought to let us know when a-sailing they
would go
So very, very early in the morning."

When every little wave has its nightcap on,
Its nightcap, white cap, nightcap on,
When every little wave has its nightcap on,
So very, very early in the morning.

Just then, up jumped the sun, and the fishes every one
For their laziness at once fell a-mourning.
But I stayed to hear no more, for my boat had reached
the shore,
So very, very early in the morning.

And every little wave took its nightcap off,
  Its nightcap, white cap, nightcap off,
And every little wave took its nightcap off,
  And curtsied to the sun in the morning.

Laura E. Richards

COME UNTO THESE YELLOW SANDS

Come unto these yellow sands,
And then take hands:
Curtsied when you have and kiss'd,
The wild waves whist,
Foot it featly here and there;
And, sweet sprites, the burden bear.
Hark, Hark!
Bow-wow
The watch-dogs bark:
Bow-wow.
Hark, hark! I hear
The strain of strutting chanticleer
Cry, Cock-a-diddle-dow.

William Shakespeare
From "The Tempest"

THE SAD STORY OF A LITTLE BOY THAT CRIED

Once a little boy, Jack, was, oh! ever so good,
Till he took a strange notion to cry all he could.

So he cried all the day, and he cried all the night,
He cried in the morning and in the twilight;

He cried till his voice was as hoarse as a crow,
And his mouth grew so large it looked like a great O.

It grew at the bottom, it grew at the top;
It grew till they thought it never would stop.

Each day his great mouth grew taller and taller,
And his dear little self grew smaller and smaller.

At last that same mouth grew so big that– alack!–
It was only a mouth with a border of Jack.

Mary Mapes Dodge

AN ALPHABET

A
A was once an apple pie,
Pidy
Widy
Tidy
Pidy
Nice insidy
Apple Pie!

B
B was once a little bear,
Beary!
Wary!
Hairy!
Beary!
Taky cary!
Little Bear!

C
C was once a little cake,
Caky
Baky
Maky
Caky
Taky Caky,
Little Cake!

continued on next page

D

D was once a little doll,
Dolly
Molly
Polly
Nolly
Nursy Dolly
Little Doll!

E

E was once a little eel,
Eely
Weely
Peely
Eely
Twirly, Tweely
Little Eel!

F

F was once a little fish,
Fishy
Wishy
Squishy
Fishy
In a Dishy
Little Fish!

G

G was once a little goose,
Goosy
Moosy
Boosey
Goosey
Waddly-woosy
Little Goose!

H

H was once a little hen,
Henny
Chenny
Tenny
Henny
Eggsy-any
Little Hen?

I

I was once a bottle of ink,
Inky
Dinky
Thinky
Inky
Blacky Minky
Bottle of Ink!

continued on next page

J

J was once a jar of jam,
Jammy
Mammy
Clammy
Jammy
Sweety–Swammy
Jar of Jam!

K

K was once a little kite,
Kity
Whity
Flighty
Kity
Out of Sighty–
Little Kite!

L

L was once a little lark,
Larky!
Marky!
Harky!
Larky!
In the Parky,
Little Lark!

M

M was once a little mouse,
Mousey
Bousey
Sousy
Mousy
In the Housy
Little Mouse!

N

N was once a little needle,
Needly
Tweedly
Threedly
Needly
Wisky–wheedly
Little Needle!

O

O was once a little owl,
Owly
Prowly
Howly
Owly
Browny fowly
Little Owl!

continued on next page

P

P was once a little pump,
Pumpy
Slumpy
Flumpy
Pumpy
Dumpy, Thumpy
Little Pump!

Q

Q was once a little quail,
Quaily
Faily
Daily
Quaily
Stumpy-taily
Little Quail!

R

R was once a little rose,
Rosy
Posy
Nosy
Rosy
Blows-y–grows-y
Little Rose!

S

S was once a little shrimp,
Shrimpy
Nimpy
Flimpy
Shrimpy
Jumpy–jimpy
Little Shrimp!

T

T was once a little thrush,
Thrushy!
Hushy!
Bushy!
Thrushy!
Flitty–Flushy
Little Thrush!

U

U was once a little urn,
Urny
Burny
Turny
Urny
Bubbly–burny
Little Urn!

continued on next page

V

V was once a little vine,
Viny
Winy
Twiny
Viny
Twisty-twiny
Little Vine!

W

W was once a whale,
Whaly
Scaly
Shaly
Whaly
Tumbly-taily
Mighty Whale!

X

X was once a great king Xerxes,
Xerxy
Perxy
Turxy
Xerxy
Linxy Lurxy
Great King Xerxes!

Y

Y was once a little yew,
Yewdy
Fewdy
Crudy
Yewdy
Growdy, grewdy,
Little Yew!

Z

Z was once a piece of zinc,
Tinky
Winky
Blinky
Tinky
Tinkly Minky
Piece of Zinc!

Edward Lear

GREAT, WIDE, BEAUTIFUL, WONDERFUL WORLD

Great, wide, beautiful, wonderful World,
With the wonderful water round you curled,
And the wonderful grass upon your breast–
World, you are beautifully drest.

The wonderful air is over me,
And the wonderful wind is shaking the tree,
It walks on the water, and whirls the mills,
And talks to itself on the tops of the hills.

You friendly earth! how far do you go,
With the wheat-fields that nod and the rivers that flow,
With cities and gardens, and cliffs, and isles,
And people upon you for thousands of miles?

Ah, you are so great and I am so small,
I tremble to think of you, World, at all;
And yet, when I said my prayers to-day,
A whisper inside me seemed to say,
"You are more than the earth, though you are such a dot:
You can love and think, and the earth cannot!"

William Brighty Rands

THE SLEEP SONG

Hush, little Baby, don't you cry!
You'll be a big girl by and by.
All the beautiful world is thine,
For thee the sun and the moon shall shine,
The stars come out and the soft winds blow,
The birds shall sing and the sweet flowers grow.
You shall be happy every day,
For mother is with you all the way.
Hush, little Baby, don't you cry!
You'll be a big girl by and by.
Hush, little birdie–peep, dear, peep!
Mother is near you–sleep, dear, sleep!

M. Nightingale

ROBIN REDBREAST

The owl that hoots in the elder-tree
I love, and the lark at dawn;
And the starling that comes to waken me,
And the thrushes that run on the lawn.

The cluck of the fowls and the pigeons' coo,
And the sparrows upon the wall;
But the robin I love till it hurts–I do!
I love him the best of all.

M. Nightingale

CATCHING FAIRIES

They're sleeping beneath the roses;
Oh! kiss them before they rise,
And tickle their tiny noses,
And sprinkle the dew on their eyes.
Make haste, make haste;
The fairies are caught,
Make haste.

We'll put them in silver cages,
And send them full-drest to court,
And maids of honour and pages
Shall turn the poor things to sport.
Be quick, be quick;
Be quicker than thought,
Be quick.

They'll scatter sweet scents by winking,
With sparks from under their feet;
They'll save us the trouble of thinking,
Their voices will sound so sweet.
Oh stay, oh stay;
They're up and away,
Oh stay!

William Cory

CATCHING FAIRIES

NIGHT AND DAY

NIGHT AND DAY

When the golden day is done,
   Through the closing portal,
Child and garden, flower and sun,
   Vanish all things mortal.

As thc blinding shadows fall,
   As the rays diminish,
Under evening's cloak they all
   Roll away and finish.

Garden darkened, daisy shut,
   Child in bed, they slumber–
Glow-worm in the highway rut,
   Mice among the lumber.

In the darkness houses shine,
   Parents move with candles,
Till on all, the night divine
   Turns the bedroom handles.

Till at last the day begins
   In the east a-breaking,
In the hedges and the whins
   Sleeping birds a-waking.

continued on next page

In the darkness shapes of things,
  Houses, trees, and hedges,
Clearer grow, and sparrows' wings
  Beat on window ledges.

These shall wake the yawning maid;
  She the door shall open–
Finding dew on garden glade
  And the morning broken.

There my garden grows again
  Green and rosy painted,
As at eve behind the pane
  From my eyes it fainted.

Just as it was shut away,
  Toy-like, in the even,
Here I see it glow with day
  Under glowing heaven.

Every path and every plot,
  Every bush of roses,
Every blue forget-me-not
  Where the dew reposes.

"Up!" they cry, "the day is come
On the smiling valleys;
We have beat the morning drum,
Playmate, join your allies!"

Robert Louis Stevenson

A LULLABY

Sleep, baby, sleep!
Thy father guards the sheep;
Thy mother shakes the dreamland tree,
Down falls a little dream for thee:
Sleep, baby, sleep!

Sleep, baby, sleep!
The large stars are the sheep;
The little stars are the lambs, I guess;
And the gentle moon is the shepherdess:
Sleep, baby, sleep!

Anonymous

FROM A RAILWAY CARRIAGE

Faster than fairies, faster than witches,
Bridges and houses, hedges and ditches;
And charging along like troops in a battle,
All through the meadows the horses and cattle:
All of the sights of the hill and the plain
Fly as thick as driving rain;
And ever again, in the wink of an eye,
Painted stations whistle by.

Here is a child who clambers and scrambles,
All by himself and gathering brambles;
Here is a tramp who stands and gazes;
And there is the green for stringing the daisies!
Here is a cart run away in the road
Lumping along with man and load;
And here is a mill, and there is a river:
Each a glimpse and gone for ever!

Robert Louis Stevenson

THE ROOKS

The rooks are building on the trees;
  They build there every spring:
'Caw, caw,' is all they say,
  For none of them can sing.

They're up before the break of day,
  And up till late at night;
For they must labour busily
  As long as it is light.

And many a crooked stick they bring,
  And many a slender twig,
And many a tuft of moss, until
  Their nests are round and big,

'Caw, caw.' Oh, what a noise
  They make in rainy weather!
Good children always speak by turns,
  But rooks all talk together.

Aunt Effie

MATILDA

Matilda told such dreadful lies,
It made one gasp and stretch one's eyes;
Her Aunt, who, from her earliest youth,
Had kept a strict regard for truth,
Attempted to believe Matilda:
The effort very nearly killed her,
And would have done so, had not she
Discovered this infirmity.
For once, towards the close of day,
Matilda, growing tired of play,
And finding she was left alone,
Went tiptoe to the telephone
And summoned the immediate aid
Of London's noble fire-brigade.
Within an hour the gallant band
Were pouring in on every hand,
From Putney, Hackney Downs, and Bow
With courage high and hearts a-glow
They galloped, roaring through the town,
'Matilda's house is burning down!'
Inspired by British cheers and loud
Proceeding from the frenzied crowd,
They ran their ladders through a score
Of windows on the ballroom floor;

And took peculiar pains to souse
The pictures up and down the house,
Until Matilda's Aunt succeeded
In showing them they were not needed;
And even then she had to pay
To get the men to go away!
It happened that a few weeks later
Her Aunt was off to the theatre
To see that interesting play
The Second Mrs. Tanqueray,
She had refused to take her niece
To hear this entertaining piece:
A deprivation just and wise
To punish her for telling lies.
That night a fire *did* break out–
You should have heard Matilda shout!
You should have heard her scream and bawl,
And throw the window up and call
To people passing in the street–
(The rapidly increasing heat
Encouraging her to obtain
Their confidence)–but all in vain!
For every time she shouted 'Fire!'
They only answered 'Little liar!'
And therefore when her Aunt returned,
Matilda, and the house, were burned.

Hilaire Belloc

AT THE ZOO

First I saw the white bear, then I saw the black;
Then I saw the camel with a hump upon his back;
Then I saw the grey wolf, with mutton in his maw;
Then I saw the wombat waddle in the straw;
Then I saw the elephant a-waving of his trunk;
Then I saw the monkeys–mercy, how unpleasantly they–smelt!

William Makepeace Thackeray

MEET-ON-THE-ROAD

"Now, pray, where are you going?" said Meet-on-the-Road.
"To school, sir, to school, sir," said Child-as-it-Stood.

"What have you in your basket, child?" said Meet-on-the-Road.
"My dinner, sir, my dinner, sir," said Child-as-it-Stood.

"What have you for dinner, child?" said Meet-on-the-Road.

"Some pudding, sir, some pudding, sir," said Child-
as-it-Stood.

"Oh, then, I pray, give me a share," said Meet-on-
the-Road.
"I've little enough for myself, sir," said Child-as-it-
Stood.

"What have you got that cloak on for?" said Meet-on-
the-Road.
"To keep the wind and cold from me," said Child-as-
it-Stood.

"I wish the wind would blow through you," said
Meet-on-the-Road.
"Oh, what a wish! What a wish!" said Child-as-it-
Stood.

"Pray, what are those bells ringing for?" said Meet-
on-the-Road.
"To ring bad spirits home again," said Child-as-it-
Stood.

"Oh, then I must be going, child!" said Meet-on-the-
Road.
"So fare you well, so fare you well," said Child-as-it-
Stood.

Anonymous

WEATHERS

This is the weather the cuckoo likes,
  And so do I;
When showers betumble the chestnut spikes,
  And nestlings fly:
And the little brown nightingale bills his best,
And they sit outside at *The Traveller's Rest*,
And maids come forth sprig-muslin drest,
And citizens dream of the south and west,
  And so do I.

This is the weather the shepherd shuns,
  And so do I:
When beeches drip in browns and duns,
  And thresh, and ply;
And hill-hid tides throb, throe on throe,
And meadow rivulets overflow,
And drops on gate-bars hang in a row,
And rooks in families homeward go,
  And so do I.

Thomas Hardy

THE COWARDLY WREN

The wren stood on a little bough,
  A-learning how to fly.
A frown was on her feathered brow,
  A tear-drop dimmed her eye!
And in a fearsome plight she stood,
  While her unspoken thought
Was, "There! it's not the slightest good;
  My wings are much too short!

"Father, could you your offspring see,
  You would not treat her so!"
Her father answered not, for he
  Was eating worms below.
"Oh, mother, listen to my cry,
  You would not be unkind!"
Her mother gave her for reply
  A gentle push behind!

There came a sudden chirp of fright;
  The wren, oh, where was she?
She'd taken an unwilling flight
  From that old apple-tree;

And sitting gasping on the ground,
  Her breath entirely spent,
Confessed, with pride, that she had found
  A new accomplishment!

Blanche Winder

THERE WAS A NAUGHTY BOY

There was a naughty boy,
A naughty boy was he,
He would not stop at home,
He could not quiet be–
He took
In his knapsack
A book
Full of vowels
And a shirt
With some towels,
A slight cap
For night cap,
A hair brush,
Comb ditto,
New stockings–
For old ones
Would split O!
This knapsack
Tight at 's back
He rivetted close
And followed his nose
To the North,
To the North,
And followed his nose
To the North.

There was a naughty boy,
  And a naughty boy was he,
He ran away to Scotland
  The people for to see–
    There he found
    That the ground
    Was as hard,
    That a yard
    Was as long,
    That a song
    Was as merry,
    That a cherry
    Was as red–
    That lead
    Was as weighty
    That fourscore
    Was as eighty,
    That a door
    Was as wooden
    As in England–
  So he stood in his shoes
    And he wondered,
    He wondered,
  He stood in his shoes
    And he wondered.

John Keats

THE TYGER

Tyger! Tyger! burning bright
In the forests of the night,
What immortal hand or eye
Could frame thy fearful symmetry?

In what distant deeps or skies
Burnt the fire of thine eyes?
On what wings dare he aspire?
What the hand dare seize the fire?

And what shoulder and what art,
Could twist the sinews of thy heart?
And when thy heart began to beat,
What dread hand? and what dread feet?

What the hammer? what the chain?
In what furnace was thy brain?
What the anvil? what dread grasp
Dare its deadly terrors clasp?

When the stars threw down their spears,
And water'd heaven with their tears,
Did he smile his work to see?
Did he who made the Lamb make thee?

Tyger! Tyger! burning bright
In the forests of the night,
What immortal hand or eye
Dare frame thy fearful symmetry?

William Blake

THE BUBBLE

Baby blew a bubble,
Softly let it fall
Like a rainbow fairy,
In a silver ball;
"Pretty little bubble,
Will you stop and play?"
But the bubble, bubble, bubbled,
Bubbled right away!

Baby blew a bubble,
Very hard she tried,
Saw another baby
Like herself inside;
"Pretty little bubble,
Will you stop and play?"
But the bubble, bubble, bubbled,
Bubbled right away!

Florence Hoatson

A PATTERN BABY

When people come to call and tell
About their babies, dear me, well–

I sit and listen all the while
And smile myself a little smile.

If mine were like some people's, there,
I would not keep her, I declare!

Their babies scream and cry and fret,
Won't eat or sleep, while my dear pet

She *never* cries; she'll stay for hours
Just looking at the birds and flowers.

The sweetest little cot has she,
All pink and white, as smart can be.

And when at night I lay her in it
She shuts her eyes in half a minute.

That all the babies in the city
Are not like mine I think a pity.

The only thing is, mine won't grow–
She is a baby doll, you know.

E. A. Mayo

A PATTERN BABY

A BOY'S SONG

A BOY'S SONG

Where the pools are bright and deep,
Where the grey trout lies asleep,
Up the river and over the lea,
That's the way for Billy and me.

Where the blackbird sings the latest,
Where the hawthorn blooms the sweetest,
Where the nestlings chirp and flee,
That's the way for Billy and me.

Where the mowers mow the cleanest,
Where the hay lies thick and greenest,
There to track the homeward bee,
That's the way for Billy and me.

Where the hazel bank is steepest,
Where the shadow falls the deepest,
Where the clustering nuts fall free,
That's the way for Billy and me.

Why the boys should drive away
Little sweet maidens from the play,
Or love to banter and fight so well,
That's the thing I never could tell.

continued on next page

But this I know, I love to play
Through the meadow, among the hay;
Up the water and over the lea,
That's the way for Billy and me.

James Hogg

GOOD NIGHT AND GOOD MORNING

A fair little girl sat under a tree,
Sewing as long as her eyes could see;
Then smoothed her work, and folded it right,
And said, "Dear work! Good Night! Good Night!"

Such a number of rooks came over her head,
Crying "Caw! caw!" on their way to bed:
She said as she watched their curious flight,
"Little black things! Good Night! Good Night!"

The horses neighed, and the oxen lowed;
The sheep's "Bleat! bleat!" came over the road;
All seeming to say, with a quiet delight,
"Good little girl! Good Night! Good Night!"

She did not say to the Sun "Good Night!"
Though she saw him there like a ball of light;
She knew he had God's time to keep
All over the world, and never could sleep.

The tall pink foxglove bowed his head,
The violets curtsied and went to bed;
And good little Lucy tied up her hair,
And said, on her knees, her favourite prayer.

And while on her pillow she softly lay,
She knew nothing more till again it was day,
And all things said to the beautiful Sun,
"Good Morning! Good Morning! our work is begun."

Lord Houghton

FLOWER FANCIES

Lily, fair Lily,
Why are you all in white?
"Child, I was born of the pale moonlight:
Where it fell through the night
Dank and chilly,
And touched with splendour the dreaming earth,
There had I birth."

continued on next page

Tall Sunflower,
Where got you your disk of yellow?
"From the golden sun that laughed as I leapt
To greet him king without fellow!
"Come, children all, to bed!" he cried;
And ere the leaves could urge their prayer
He shook his head, and far and wide,
Fluttering and nestling everywhere,
Down sped the leaflets through the air.

I saw them; on the ground they lay,
Golden and red, a huddled swarm,
Waiting, till one from far away,
White bedclothes heaped upon her arm,
Should come to wrap them safe and warm.

The great bare Tree looked down and smiled.
"Good night, dear little leaves," he said;
And from below each sleepy child
Replied, "Good night," and murmured,
"It is so nice to go to bed."

Susan Coolidge

THE COW

The friendly cow, all red and white,
I love with all my heart:
She gives me cream with all her might,
To eat with apple tart.

She wanders lowing here and there,
And yet she cannot stray,
All in the pleasant open air,
The pleasant light of day;

And blown by all the winds that pass
And wet with all the showers,
She walks among the meadow grass
And eats the meadow flowers.

Robert Louis Stevenson

MEG MERRILIES

Old Meg she was a gipsy,
And lived upon the moors;
Her bed it was the brown heath turf,
And her house was out of doors.
Her apples were swart blackberries,
Her currants, pods o'broom;
Her wine was dew of the wild white rose,
Her book a churchyard tomb.

Her brothers were the craggy hills,
Her sisters larchen trees;
Alone with her great family
She lived as she did please.
No breakfast had she many a morn,
No dinner many a noon,
And, 'stead of supper, she would stare
Full hard against the moon.

But every morn, of woodbine fresh
She made her garlanding;
And, every night, the dark glen yew
She wove, and she would sing.
And with her fingers, old and brown,
She plaited mats of rushes,
And gave them to the cottagers
She met among the bushes.

Old Meg was brave as Margaret Queen,
And tall as Amazon:
An old red blanket cloak she wore,
A chip-hat had she on.
God rest her aged bones somewhere–
She died full long agone!

John Keats

TRUTH THE BEST

Yesterday Rebecca Mason,
In the parlour by herself,
Broke a handsome china basin,
Placed upon the mantelshelf.

Quite alarmed, she thought of going
Very quietly away,
Not a single person knowing
Of her being there that day.

But Rebecca recollected
She was taught deceit to shun;
And the moment she reflected,
Told her mother what was done;

Who commended her behaviour,
Loved her better, and forgave her.

Elizabeth Turner

SIR PATRICK SPENS

I. The Sailing

The king sits in Dunfermline town,
Drinking the blude-red wine;
"O whar will I get a skeely skipper
To sail this new ship o'mine?"

Up and spak an eldern knight,
Sat at the king's right knee:
"Sir Patrick Spens is the best sailor
That ever sail'd the sea."

Our king has written a braid letter,
And seal'd it wi' his hand,
And sent it to Sir Patrick Spens,
Was walking on the strand.

"To Noroway, to Noroway,
To Noroway o'er the faem;
The king's daughter o' Noroway,
'Tis thou maun bring her hame."

The first word that Sir Patrick read
A loud laugh laughed he;
The neist word that Sir Patrick read,
The tear blinded his e'e.

"O wha is this has done this deed
And tauld the king o'me,
To send us out, at this time o'year,
To sail upon the sea?

"Be it wind, be it weet, be it hail, be it sleet,
Our ship must sail the faem;
The king's daughter o' Noroway,
'Tis we maun fetch her hame."

They hoysed their sails on Monenday morn
Wi' a' the speed they may;
They ha'e landed in Noroway
Upon a Wodensday.

II. The Return

"Mak ready, mak ready, my merry men a'!
Our gude ship sails the morn."–
"Now ever alack, my master dear,
I fear a deadly storm!

"I saw the new moon late yestreen
Wi' the auld moon in her arm;
And if we gang to sea, master,
I fear we'll come to harm!"

continued on next page

They hadna' sailed a league, a league,
A league but barely three,
When the lift grew dark, and the wind blew loud,
And gurly grew the sea.

The anchors brak, and the topmast lap
It was sic a deadly storm;
And the waves cam owre the broken ship
Till a' her sides were torn.

"O whar will I get a gude sailor
To tak my helm in hand,
Till I get up to the tall topmast
To see if I can spy land?"–

"Oh here am I, a sailor gude,
To tak the helm in hand,
Till you go up to the tall topmast,
But I fear you'll ne'er spy land."

He hadna game a step, a step,
A step but barely ane,
When a bolt flew out of our goodly ship,
And the saut sea it came in.

"Gae fetch a web o' the silken claith,
  Another o' the twine,
And wap them into our ship's side,
  And let na' the sea come in."

They fetched a web o' the silken claith,
  Another o' the twine,
And they wrapped them round that gude ship's side,
  But still the sea cam in.

O laith, laith were our gude Scots lords
  To wet their cork-heel'd shoon;
But lang or a' the play was play'd
  They wet their hats aboon.

And mony was the feather bed
  That flatter'd on the faem;
And mony was the gude laird's son
  That never mair cam hame.

O lang, lang may the ladies sit,
  Wi' their fans into their hand,
Before they see Sir Patrick Spens
  Come sailing to thc strand!

continued on next page

And lang, lang may the maidens sit
  Wi' their gowd kames in their hair,
A' waiting for their ain dear loves!
  For them they'll see nae mair.

Half-owre, half-owre to Aberdour,
  'Tis fifty fathoms deep;
And there lies gude Sir Patrick Spens
  Wi' the Scots lords at his feet!

Anonymous

Skeely, skilful; *braid,* plain; *faem,* foam; *maun,* must; *neist,* net; *hoysed,* hoisted; *lift,* sky; *gurly,* stormy; *lap,* sprang; *saut,* salt; *claith,* cloth; *wap,* wrap; *laith,* unwilling; *kames,* combs.

WHAT MIGHT HAVE BEEN

The little birds are singing
  Above their speckled eggs,
The daddy-long-legs talks about
  His children's lovely legs.

The red cow thinks her little calf
  The best that there can be,
And my papa and my mamma
  Are very proud of me!

And yet I might have been a bird,
  And slept within a nest,
Or been a daddy-long-legs
  With scarcely any chest;

Or been a little calf or pig,
  And grown to beef or ham;
I'm very, very, very glad
  That I am what I am!

Fred E. Weatherly

THE THINGS BEHIND THE TREES

It's the things behind the trees I don't like very much,
The shadows and the moving things, the whisp'ring things and such,
They make you feel as if they watch and murmur in the air:
"Now *you* take care!"

The sun is warm and jolly and he shines on all he sees,
I don't believe *he* likes the things that hide behind the trees,
Yet if you walk straight up to them and peep behind with care–
They're never there!
And I wouldn't mind them half so much
If they were!

Dorothy Dickinson

A JAPANESE LULLABY

Sleep, sleep, on the floor, oh! be good and slumber;
For when thou art asleep
Just hear what I shall do, dear.

Far o'er the mountain will I go and buy thee
All sorts of pretty toys
And bring them home to baby.

And when thou early wak'st to-morrow morning,
Thou shalt eat red beans
And fish, my baby.

From "Cradle Songs of Many Nations"

INFANT JOY

"I have no name;
I am but two days old."
–What shall I call thee?
"I happy am;
Joy is my name."
–Sweet joy befall thee!

Pretty joy!
Sweet joy, but two days old:
Sweet joy I call thee:
Thou dost smile:
I sing the while,
Sweet joy befall thee!

William Blake

INFANT JOY

A JAPANESE LULLABY

THE LOBSTER

THE LOST DOLL

THE LOST DOLL

I once had a sweet little doll, dears,
The prettiest doll in the world;
Her cheeks were so red and so white, dears,
And her hair was so charmingly curled.
But I lost my poor little doll, dears,
As I played in the heath one day;
And I cried for her more than a week, dears,
But I never could find where she lay.

I found my poor little doll, dears,
As I played in the heath one day;
Folks say she is terribly changed, dears,
For her paint is all washed away,
And her arm trodden off by the cows, dears,
And her hair not the least bit curled:
Yet for old sakes' sake she is still, dears
The prettiest doll in the world.

Charles Kingsley
From "The Water Babies"

THE LOBSTER

He was a gentle lobster
  (The boats had just come in)–
He did not love the fishermen,
  He could not stand their din;
And so he quietly stole off,
  As if it were no sin.

She was a little maiden,
  He met her on the sand,
"And how d'you do?" the lobster said;
  "Why don't you give your hand?"
For why she edged away from him
  He *could* not understand.

"Excuse me, sir," the maiden said,
  "Excuse me, if you please,"
And put her hands behind her back,
  And doubled up her knees;
"I always thought that lobsters were
  A little apt to squeeze."

"Your ignorance," the lobster said,
"Is natural, I fear;
Such scandal is a shame," he sobbed,
"It is not true, my dear!"
And with his pocket handkerchief
He wiped away a tear.

So out she put her little hand,
As though she feared him not,
When someone grabbed him suddenly,
And put him in a pot,
With water which, I think, he found
Uncomfortably hot.

It may have been the water made
The blood flow to his head,
It may have been that dreadful fib
Lay on his soul like lead:
This much is true–he went in grey
And came out very red.

Fred E. Weatherly

THE POBBLE WHO HAS NO TOES

The Pobble who has no toes
  Had once as many as we;
When they said, "Some day you may lose them all"–
  He replied, "Fish fiddle de-dee!"
And his Aunt Jobiska made him drink,
Lavender water tinged with pink,
For she said, "The World in general knows
There's nothing so good for a Pobble's toes!"

The Pobble who has no toes,
  Swam across the Bristol Channel;
But before he set out he wrapped his nose,
  In a piece of scarlet flannel.
For his Aunt Jobiska said, 'No harm
Can come to his toes if his nose is warm;
And it's perfectly known that a Pobble's toes
Are safe–provided he minds his nose.'

The Pobble swam fast and well
  And when boats or ships came near him
He tinkledy-binkledy-winkled a bell
  So that all the world could hear him.
And all the Sailors and Admirals cried,
When they saw him nearing the further side–
"He has gone to fish, for his Aunt Jobiska's
Runcible Cat with crimson whiskers!"

But before he touched the shore,
  The shore of the Bristol Channel,
A sea-green Porpoise carried away
  His wrapper of scarlet flannel.
And when he came to observe his feet
Formerly garnished with toes so neat
His face at once became forlorn
On perceiving that all his toes were gone!

And nobody ever knew
  From that dark day to the present,
Whoso had taken the Pobble's toes,
  In a manner so far from pleasant.
Whether the shrimps or crawfish grey,
Or crafty Mermaids stole them away–
Nobody knew; and nobody knows
How the Pobble was robbed of his twice five toes!

The Pobble who has no toes
  Was placed in a friendly Bark,
And they rowed him back, and carried him up,
  To his Aunt Jobiska's Park.
And she made him a feast at his earnest wish
Of eggs and buttercups fried with fish–
And she said, "It's a fact the whole world knows,
That Pobbles are happier without their toes."

Edward Lear

THE KITTEN AND THE FALLING LEAVES

See the Kitten on the wall,
Sporting with the leaves that fall,
Withered leaves – one-two-and three–
From the lofty elder-tree!
Through the calm and frosty air
Of this morning bright and fair,
Eddying round and round they sink
Softly, slowly: one might think,
From the motions that are made,
Every little leaf conveyed
Sylph or Faery hither tending,
To this lower world descending,
Each invisible and mute
In his wavering parachute.

– But the Kitten, how she starts,
Crouches, stretches, paws, and darts!
First at one, and then its fellow
Just as light and just as yellow.
There are many now – now one –
Now they stop and there are none:
What intenseness of desire
In her upward eye of fire!

With a tiger-leap half-way
Now she meets the coming prey,
Lets it go as fast, and then
Has it in her power again:
Now she works with three or four,
Like an Indian conjurer;
Quick as he in feats of art,
Far beyond in joy of heart.
Were her antics played in the eye
Of a thousand standers-by,
Clapping hands with shout and stare,
What would little Tabby care
For the plaudits of the crowd?

William Wordsworth

WHERE THE BEE SUCKS

Where the bee sucks, there suck I,
In a cowslip's bell I lie,
There I couch when owls do cry.
On the bat's back I do fly
After summer merrily.
Merrily, merrily shall I live now
Under the blossom that hangs on the bough.

William Shakespeare

THE BROOK

I come from haunts of coot and hern,
  I make a sudden sally,
And sparkle out among the fern,
  To bicker down a valley.

By thirty hills I hurry down,
  Or slip between the ridges,
By twenty thorps, a little town,
  And half a hundred bridges.

Till last by Philip's farm I flow
  To join the brimming river,
For men may come and men may go,
  But I go on for ever.

I chatter over stony ways,
  In little sharps and trebles,
I bubble into eddying bays,
  I babble on the pebbles.

With many a curve my banks I fret
  By many a field and fallow,
And many a fairy foreland set
  With willow-weed and mallow.

I chatter, chatter, as I flow
To join the brimming river,
For men may come and men may go,
But I go on for ever.

I wind about, and in and out,
With here a blossom sailing,
And here and there a lusty trout,
And here and there a grayling.

And here and there a foamy flake
Upon me, as I travel
With many a silvery waterbreak
Above the golden gravel.

And draw them all along, and flow
To join the brimming river,
For men may come and men may go,
But I go on for ever.

I steal by lawns and grassy plots,
I slide by hazel covers;
I move the sweet forget-me-nots
That grow for happy lovers.

continued on next page

I slip, I slide, I gloom, I glance,
Among my skinning swallows;
I make the netted sunbeam dance
Against my sandy shallows.

I murmur under moon and stars
In brambly wildernesses;
I linger by my shingly bars;
I loiter round my cresses;

And out again I curve and flow
To join the brimming river,
For men may come and men may go,
But I go on for ever.

Alfred, Lord Tennyson

FISHERMAN'S LORE

When the wind is in the East
'Tis neither good for man nor beast.

When the wind is in the North
The skilful fisher goes not forth.

When the wind is in the South
It blows the bait in the fish's mouth.

When the wind is in the West,
Then it is at its very best.

Anonymous

LITTLE TROTTY WAGTAIL

Little trotty wagtail, he went in the rain,
And tittering, tottering sideways he ne'er got straight
again,
He stooped to get a worm, and looked up to catch a fly,
And then he flew away ere his feathers they were dry.

Little trotty wagtail, he waddled in the mud,
And left his little footmarks, trample where he would.
He waddled in the water-pudge, and waggle went his
tail,
And chirrupt up his wings to dry upon the garden rail.

Little trotty wagtail, you nimble all about,
And in the dimpling water-pudge you waddle in and
out;
Your home is nigh at hand, and in the warm pigsty,
So, little Master Wagtail, I'll bid you a good-bye.

John Clare

THE MOCK TURTLE'S SONG

"Will you walk a little faster?" said a
  whiting to a snail,
"There's a porpoise close behind us, and he's
  treading on my tail.
See how eagerly the lobsters and the turtles all
  advance!
They are waiting on the shingle–will you come
  and join the dance?
Will you, won't you, will you, won't you, will
  you join the dance?
Will you, won't you, will you, won't you, won't
  you join the dance?

"You can really have no notion how delightful
  it will be
When they take us up and throw us, with the
  lobsters, out to sea!"
But the snail replied, "Too far, too far!" and
  gave a look askance–
Said he thanked the whiting kindly, but he
  would not join the dance.
Would not, could not, would not, could not,
  would not join the dance.
Would not, could not, would not, could not,
  could not join the dance.

"What matters is how far we go?" his scaly
friend replied,
"There is another shore, you know, upon the
other side.
The further off from England the nearer is to
France–
Then turn not pale, beloved snail, but come and
join the dance.
Will you, won't you, will you, won't you, will
you join the dance?
Will you, won't you, will you, won't you, won't
you join the dance?"

Lewis Carroll
"Alice in Wonderland"

A CHINESE BABY SONG

Snail, snail, come out and be fed,
Put out your horns, and then your head,
And your Papa and your Mamma
Will give you boiled mutton.

Anonymous

THE DREAM TOWN TRAIN

When little feet grow weary,
  And the toys are packed away,
And drowsy lids are closing
  Over blue eyes, brown, and grey,
Each night from Blanket Station,
  In the Realm of Counterpane,
The children take their tickets for
  The dream town train!

It starts at half-past bedtime
  By the station clock, you'll find,
And late or naughty children
  Are, of course, all left behind;
They hear the guard's loud whistle,
  And they cry, "Please wait!" in vain,
While the good ones go without them by
  The dream town train!

For miles and miles they travel
  Past enchanted woods and streams,
By Sleeping Beauty's Palace
  To the magic Land of Dreams;
All night they feast and frolic
  Till the sun wakes up again,
Then home they come from Dreamland in
  The dream town train!

So hasten, all good children,
  If you'd see that land so fair,
Its wonders and its treasures,
  And its castles in the air;
Just take the road at bedtime
  To the Realm of Counterpane,
And wait at Blanket Station for
  The dream town train!

Mary Farrah

SEVEN TIMES ONE

There's no dew left on the daisies and clover,
There's no rain left in heaven:
I've said my "seven times" over and over,
Seven times one are seven.

I am old, so old I can write a letter;
My birthday lessons are done;
The lambs play always, they know no better;
They are only one times one.

O velvet Bee, you're a dusty fellow,
You've powdered your legs with gold!
O brave Marsh Marybuds, rich and yellow,
Give me your money to hold!

And show me your nest, with the young ones in it;
I will not steal them away;
I am old! you may trust me, linnet, linnet,–
I am seven times one to-day.

Jean Ingelow

SEVEN TIMES ONE

SING A SONG OF MORNING

SING A SONG OF MORNING

Sing a song of morning,
  Sunshine bright outside,
Roscs at thc window,
  Blue eyes opening wide,
Sound of water splashing,
  Hair well brushed and neat,
Breakfast on the table,
  Mother's smile so sweet.

Sing a song of schooltime,
  Fun the road along,
Merry comrades marching
  All in time to song,
Teacher's kindly greeting,
  Work well done, sums right,
Every scholar's motto,
  "Try with all your might."

Sing a song of evening,
  Birds that homeward fly,
Roses pale as silver
  'Neath the twilight sky,
Little prayers low whispered,
  Heads on pillows white,
Kisses for dear mother–
  Sleep till morning's light.

Augusta Hancock

NANCY'S NIGHTMARE

I am the doll that Nancy broke!
  Hadn't been hers a week.
One little squeeze, and I sweetly spoke;
  Rosy and fair was my cheek.
Now my head lies in a corner far,
  My body lies here in the other;
And if this is what human children are.
  I never will live with another!

I am the book that Nancy read
  For fifteen minutes together;
Now I am standing here on my head,
  While she's gone to look at the weather.
My leaves are crushed in the cruellest way,
  There's jam on my opening page;
And I would not live with Miss Nancy Gay,
  Though I shouldn't be read for an age!

I am the frock that Nancy wore
  Last night at her birthday feast;
I am the frock that Nancy tore
  In seventeen places at least.
My buttons are scattering far and near,
  My trimming is torn to rags;
And if I were Miss Nancy's mother dear,
  I'd dress her in calico bags!

We are the words that Nancy said
  When these things were brought to her view;
All of us ought to be painted red,
  And some of us are not true.
We sputter and mutter and snarl and snap,
  We smoulder and smoke and blaze;
And if she'd not meet with some sad mishap,
  Miss Nancy must mend her ways.

Laura E. Richards

HE LOVES ME

One I Love, two I love,
Three I love I say;
Four I Love with all my heart,
Five I cast away.
Six he loves, seven she loves,
Eight they love together;
Nine he comes, ten he tarries,
Eleven he woos, and twelve he marries.

Anonymous

A SMUGGLER'S SONG

If you wake at midnight, and hear a horse's feet,
Don't go drawing back the blind, or looking in the street,
Them that asks no questions isn't told a lie.
Watch the wall, my darling, while the Gentlemen go by!
Five and twenty ponies
Trotting through the dark–
Brandy for the Parson,
'Baccy for the Clerk;
Laces for a lady, letters for a spy,
And watch the wall, my darling, while the Gentlemen go by!

Running round the woodlump if you chance to find
Little barrels, roped and tarred, all full of brandy-wine,
Don't you shout to come and look, nor use 'em for your play.
Put the brishwood back again–and they'll be gone next day!

If you see the stable-door setting open wide;
If you see a tired horse lying down inside;
If your mother mends a coat cut about and tore;
If the lining's wet and warm–don't you ask no more!

If you meet King George's men, dressed in blue and
red,
You be careful what you say, and mindful what is said.
If they call you 'pretty maid', and chuck you 'neath
the chin,
Don't you tell where no one is, nor yet where no one's
been!

Knocks and footsteps round the house–whistles after
dark–
You've no call for running out till the house-dogs bark.
Trusty's here, and *Pincher's* here, and see how dumb
they lie–
They don't fret to follow when the Gentlemen go by!

If you do as you've been told, 'likely there's a chance,
You'll be give a dainty doll, all the way from France,
With a cap of Valenciennes, and a velvet hood–
A present from the Gentlemen, along o'being good!

Five and twenty ponies,
Trotting through the dark–
Brandy for the Parson,
'Baccy for the Clerk.
Them that asks no questions isn't told a lie–
Watch the wall, my darling, while the Gentlemen go
by!

Rudyard Kipling

CASEY JONES

Come all you rounders if you want to hear
The story of a brave engineer;
Casey Jones was the hogger's name,
On a big eight-wheeler, boys, he won his fame.
Caller called Casey at half-past four,
He kissed his wife at the station door,
Mounted to the cabin with orders in his hand,
And took his farewell trip to the promised land.

Casey Jones, he mounted to the cabin,
Casey Jones, with his orders in his hand!
Casey Jones, he mounted to the cabin,
Took his farewell trip into the promised land.

"Put in your water and shovel in your coal,
Put your head out the window, watch the drivers roll,
I'll run her till she leaves the rail,
'Cause we're eight hours late with the Western Mail!"
He looked at his watch and his watch was slow,
Looked at the water and the water was low,
Turned to his fireboy and said,
"We'll get to 'Frisco, but we'll all be dead!"

Casey Jones, he mounted to the cabin,
Casey Jones, with his orders in his hand!
Casey Jones, he mounted to the cabin,
Took his farewell trip into the promised land.

Casey pulled up Reno Hill,
Tooted for the crossing with an awful shrill,
Snakes all knew by the engine's moans
That the hogger at the throttle was Casey Jones.
He pulled up short two miles from the place,
Number Four stared him right in the face,
Turned to his fireboy, said, "You'd better jump,
'Cause there's two locomotives that's going to bump."

Casey Jones, he mounted to the cabin,
Casey Jones, with his orders in his hand!
Casey Jones, he mounted to the cabin,
Took his farewell trip into the promised land.

Casey said, just before he died,
"There's two more roads I'd like to ride."
Fireboy said, "What can they be?"
"The Rio Grande and the Old S.P."
Mrs. Jones sat on her bed a-sighing,
Got a pink that Casey was dying.
Said, "Go to bed, children; hush your crying,
'Cause you'll get another papa on the Salt Lake line."

Casey Jones! Got another papa!
Casey Jones, on the Salt Lake Line!
Casey Jones! Got another papa!
Got another papa on the Salt Lake Line!

Anonymous

MEASLES IN THE ARK

The night it was horribly dark,
The measles broke out in the Ark;
Little Japheth, and Shem, and all the young Hams,
Were screaming at once for potatoes and clams.
And "What shall I do," said poor Mrs. Noah,
"All alone by myself in this terrible shower?
I know what I'll do: I'll step down in the hold,
And wake up a lioness grim and old,
And tie her close to the children's door,
And give her a ginger-cake to roar
At the top of her voice for an hour or more;
And I'll tell the children to cease their din,
Or I'll let that grim old party in,
To stop their squeazles and likewise their measles."
She practised this with the greatest success:
She was everyone's grandmother, I guess.

Susan Coolidge

THE COMMON CORMORANT

The common cormorant or shag
Lays eggs inside a paper bag
The reason you will see no doubt
It is to keep the lightning out.
But what these unobservant birds
Have never noticed is that herds
Of wandering bears may come with buns
And steal the bag to hold the crumbs.

Anonymous

RAIN IN SUMMER

How beautiful is the rain!
After the dust and heat,
In the broad and fiery street,
In the narrow lane,
How beautiful is the rain!

H. W. Longfellow

LULLABY

You spotted snakes with double tongue,
  Thorny hedgehogs, be not seen;
Newts and blind-worms, do no wrong,
  Come not near our fairy queen.

    Philomel, with melody
    Sing in our sweet lullaby;
Lulla, lulla, lullaby; lulla, lulla, lullaby:
    Never harm,
    Nor spell nor charm,
  Come our lovely lady nigh.
  So, good night, with lullaby.

Weaving spiders, come not here;
  Hence, you long-legg'd spinners, hence!
Beetles black, approach not near;
  Worm nor snail, do no offence.

    Philomel, with melody
    Sing in our sweet lullaby;
Lulla, lulla, lullaby; lulla, lulla, lullaby:
    Never harm,
    Nor spell nor charm,
  Come our lovely lady nigh.
  So, good night, with lullaby.

William Shakespeare

INDEX OF FIRST LINES